T0285998

ADVENTURES OF A TRANSPLANTED GARDENER

UNIVERSITY PRESS OF FLORIDA

Florida A&M University, Tallahassee
Florida Atlantic University, Boca Raton
Florida Gulf Coast University, Ft. Myers
Florida International University, Miami
Florida State University, Tallahassee
New College of Florida, Sarasota
University of Central Florida, Orlando
University of Florida, Gainesville
University of North Florida, Jacksonville
University of South Florida, Tampa
University of West Florida, Pensacola

Adventures of a Transplanted Gardener

Advice for New Florida Gardeners

GINNY STIBOLT

University Press of Florida

Gainesville · Tallahassee · Tampa · Boca Raton

Pensacola · Orlando · Miami · Jacksonville · Ft. Myers · Sarasota

27 26 25 24 23 22   6 5 4 3 2 1

ISBN 978-0-8130-6864-0
Library of Congress Control Number: 2021947167

The University Press of Florida is the scholarly publishing agency for the State
University System of Florida, comprising Florida A&M University, Florida Atlantic
University, Florida Gulf Coast University, Florida International University, Florida
State University, New College of Florida, University of Central Florida, University of
Florida, University of North Florida, University of South Florida, and University of
West Florida.

University Press of Florida
2046 NE Waldo Road
Suite 2100
Gainesville, FL 32609
http://upress.ufl.edu

This book is dedicated to Dean Avery,
my husband and partner in green living.

Contents

Preface

Almost a thousand people move to Florida every day. My husband, Dean Avery, and I were part of this trend when we moved to northeast Florida from Maryland in June 2004. I had looked forward to spending more time gardening, but despite my lifelong experience as a gardener and having earned an advanced degree in botany, I was flummoxed by Florida gardening. This was a humbling and unexpected series of surprises.

My Florida gardening failures were wide-ranging, but when I analyzed them, there were two main categories. In some cases my failures were due to my assumptions based on previous gardening experiences in the Mid-Atlantic and New England states, but other times, local stores were selling inappropriate plant materials. For example, I'd purchased sixty-four tulip bulbs from a local big-box store and planted them that first fall in Florida. To find out where they'd do the best, I planted some in partial shade and some in full sun. I was looking to recreate the lovely tulip gardens I had in Maryland. The next spring, only one leaf sprouted! That was it. I talked to a neighbor about this, and she said that down here, you need to put them in the fridge for six weeks and to plant them after Christmas, not in the fall. The next fall, I bought only twenty-five bulbs and followed my neighbor's instructions. The next spring, only ten tulips produced flowers—still not the impact I was looking for or expecting. And nowhere on the packaging did it say to force the bulbs in the South by cooling before planting to simulate winter. So why were the stores even offering these bulbs for sale here, when they were pretty much guaranteed to fail in Florida?

The reason for the tulip failure is that, here in North Florida where, on average, we experience six killing frosts in the winter, the soil doesn't stay cold enough for long enough. This is because in between those frosty days, it warms up into the seventies. Those wild temperature fluctuations are also hard on the gardeners. Days with forty-degree weather feel much colder here than they ever did when I lived farther north.

After a number of significant failures, I stopped assuming that I knew what I was doing and began to educate myself on what went wrong and why. It was the second category of failures, where local stores were selling inappropriate materials for our gardens that I found particularly frustrating. It occurred to me that I was probably not alone in my frustrations with Florida gardening, so I decided to share my hard-won knowledge as a community columnist for Jacksonville's *Florida Times-Union* newspaper. I called my column Adventures of a Transplanted Gardener; I wrote a new piece every two or three weeks, and they were quite popular. The paper published them in their online edition, and many were also included in the various neighborhood print editions. I wrote nearly a hundred columns over three and a half years. I also recorded more than a hundred podcasts for the paper, which sometimes amplified the topics from my columns, but anything related to plants or gardening was fair game. Of course, my learning continued as I shared my experiences with each column I wrote.

When the community columnist program ended, I continued to write articles for various organizations, for magazines, and for various blogs, including the Florida Native Plant Society's blog, and eventually, for my own *Green Gardening Matters* blog. In addition, I've written or cowritten four peer-reviewed Florida gardening books that have been published by the University Press of Florida: *Sustainable Gardening for Florida* in 2009; *Organic Methods for Vegetable Gardening in Florida* with Melissa Contreras in 2013; *The Art of Maintaining a Florida Native Landscape* in 2015, and *A Step-by-Step Guide to a Florida Native Yard* with Marjorie Shropshire in 2018. Also, I coauthored *Climate-Wise Landscaping: Practical Actions for a Sustainable Future* with Sue Reed, a landscape architect in Massachusetts, published in 2018 by New Society Publishers. Now, of course, I've written this book, and I have plans for even more books. While this seems like a lot of writing, my one consistent goal remains the same: To present doable ideas so that gardeners can be more successful and also to add more sustainability to their gardening.

My eighteen-year-old self who majored in math with minors in science and education would have been astonished that she'd become a prolific writer later in life. Maybe you can relate to a perfectly planned life that takes winding and sometimes sudden detours that lands you in surprising situations.

I would like to thank Dean Avery, Sue Dingwell, Sue Reed, Shirley Denton, and Gail Taylor, as well as two peer reviewers, for reading my manuscript or sections of the manuscript and making insightful comments and suggestions. I would also like to thank the editors and staff at the University Press of Florida for working with me to design and publish this book.

Goals for This Book

Sometimes gardening advice comes from people who clearly haven't lived through the gardening experiences they're writing about. I remember reading advice in a popular gardening magazine suggesting that planting hollies near your swimming pool is a good idea: since they are evergreen, you won't have to clear leaves out of your pool. The writer obviously had never lived with a holly, because even evergreen hollies lose their leaves, and worse, their hard spiny leaves are not fun to walk on with your bare feet. Even though I have the academic knowledge to draw on, most of the advice in this book comes from real-life lessons learned at the school of hard knocks.

I'm sharing my gardening experiences and hard-learned lessons in this book to provide gardeners transplanted to Florida a good head start. Hopefully, you can avoid some of the mistakes that I've made over the years. I have referenced some of my old columns in this book because they recorded my initial experiences, but I've updated those ideas for you with my 20–20 hindsight. While I'll be sharing my experiences to give you a head start, in the end, your own experiences in your yard, and nature itself, will be your best teachers. Some plants will work out just the way you planned, but other times they may die for no apparent reason or they might become too exuberant.

Gardening is the slowest form of performance art!

One of the best pieces of gardening advice I received was from a wholesale grower who supplies Florida natives to retail nurseries. I'd planted three bunches of Elliott's lovegrass (*Eragrostis elliottii*) at the edge of a meadow. It's an attractive, pale-green bunching grass that grows to a little more than two feet in all directions. It's native to all of Florida. I irrigated the grasses until they adjusted and thought I'd planted them in a perfect place, but they died after only a year. I knew that he had been the supplier for my local native nursery. When I saw him at a multivendor native plant sale, I asked what I should do in the future. His advice was simple. "Don't plant it there again." So, yes, heed the advice of people like me who have experience or credentials, but then listen to your own landscape, since it will have unknown factors that can influence and affect the successes or failures of your plants.

This book is not meant to be a comprehensive guide to everything in Florida; instead, it is more of a sampler of overall principles, with only one or two representative species of a plant group that I think you'd be most interested in, and with brief descriptions of only a few of Florida's many native ecosystems. I hope that this book provides a starting point for your further study or research into these topics based on your needs and your location within our beautiful state. I've arranged the topics in this book beginning with an introduction to the state and its native areas and then the reasons and resources for planting natives to help your yard become part of the "Real Florida." After that, I've ordered the topics from the easiest and most popular, like pollinator gardens, and then on to the more complex topics, like composting and storm-water management. While I think I've arranged the topics so the book is readable from front to back, each topic stands on its own, so feel free to skip around as needed.

Gardening in Florida is a wonderful year-round adventure, and as you'll find out, the seasons are really different here. I hope this book will help you adjust a bit more quickly to gardening in your new state. I know that I find peace while working with nature in our Florida yard, and I wish the same for you.

Fifty percent of the royalties for this book will be paid directly to the Florida Native Plant Society.
www.GreenGardeningMatters.com
Ginny Stibolt
Summer 2021

1

❧

Welcome to Florida

Florida is flat, really flat—with the highest altitudes reaching to only a bit more than three hundred feet above sea level in two areas of the state. One of these is in the center of peninsular Florida near Lake Wales and the other is in the Panhandle region northeast of Pensacola at the Florida-Alabama state line. But just because Florida is flat, that doesn't mean that we have a boring landscape. Florida has some amazing and unique features and a wide variety of ecosystems.

There are 1,350 miles of coastline in Florida, and 75 percent of our population lives in Florida's coastal zones. If you drove the 832 miles from Pensacola to Key West, it would take about fourteen hours with no stops. But you *would* want to stop, because there are so many wonderful attractions and assets in our state. For instance, not too far south of Florida's highest spot in the Panhandle is Falling Waters State Park, where our tallest waterfall is located. The water falls seventy-three feet—not because it falls from a high spot in the landscape, but because it falls into a deep sinkhole in the limestone rock. If you visit, go during the wet season when the water volume is greater. You would also want to stop at the Crystal River Preserve State Park on the Gulf Coast, where warm freshwater springs attract the iconic manatees in the winter. Also, you would want to stop at the Anhinga Trail in Everglades National Park, where you're sure to spot alligators basking on the shore and a wide variety of amazing birds that are so close that photographers with their huge telephoto lenses have to back up to take their pictures.

Florida has set aside many wonderfully diverse natural areas, including 3 national parks, 3 national forests, 20 national wildlife refuges, 2 national seashores, 114 state parks, 5 state forests, 3 state reserves, and 19 state preserves. The Florida Park Service is one of the largest in the country, with nearly 800,000 acres and 100 miles of beaches set aside for public access, and Florida has won the National Recreation and Park Association's Gold Medal honoring the nation's best state park system four times. From swimming and diving in Florida's rivers, springs, and coral reefs, to paddling, birding, fishing, and hiking or riding on natural scenic trails, Florida's parks and preserves offer year-round outdoor activities for all ages. Visiting Florida's natural areas will help you discover the Real Florida away from the hustle and bustle of your daily life. Setting aside time to appreciate Florida's wonderful assets could take years filled with interesting field trips.

As gardeners, knowing about Florida's local plant communities helps inform our planting choices for our yards, even if they're remote from wild spaces. So I start this introduction to Florida with short descriptions of some of Florida's wide variety of hydrological features, and then I'll cover a few examples of Florida's natural plant communities.

Florida's Natural Water Sources

With some variation through the state, the average annual rainfall is about fifty inches. As a result, Florida has a wide variety of natural water sources, which influence and interconnect local ecosystems and plant communities. Aquifers feed springs when they rise to the surface. Rivers can come from springs and flow to and through wetlands and lakes. Rivers, in turn, nourish the food webs of coastal estuaries. In the past, water has been treated like an infinite resource, but now we are finding that our bodies of water and waterways need more protections and conservation as we move into the future, if we want to leave a livable Florida for future generations.

Aquifers

Aquifers are underground networks of porous rocks that hold water and allow water to move through the holes within the rock. When aquifers intersect with the surface of the soil, they are the source for springs. The Floridan aquifer is found beneath all of Florida and portions of Alabama, Georgia, and South Carolina, plus it extends into the Gulf of Mexico and the Atlantic Ocean. This aquifer system has been divided into upper and lower aquifers separated by layers of rock or clay. There are several smaller aquifers nearer to the surface in various parts of the state. The vast majority of our drinking water comes from wells drilled into these aquifers.

Aquifers are replenished by rainwater that percolates through the soil. If more water has been siphoned from the aquifer than the replenishment rate, there may be saltwater incursions or sinkhole formations. Sinkholes can form where the rock below the land surface is limestone or other material that can be dissolved by groundwater. As the rock dissolves, spaces and caverns develop underground. The resulting terrain, called karst, is honeycombed with cavities. When a cavity becomes too big to support its ceiling, it suddenly gives way, collapsing the clay and sand above to leave a sinkhole at the surface. Sinkhole formation can be gradual or sudden, and the holes can be large or small. The western areas in North and Central Florida are more prone to sinkholes than the rest of the state, but these areas also have more springs.

To reduce the stress on the intricate system of Florida's aquifers, there will likely be more irrigation restrictions in the future as droughts increase and as our population continues to grow. As gardeners, we can help protect our aquifers by reducing our landscape irrigation rates and by not applying landscape-wide pesticides or fertilizers that could also percolate into the local aquifer. In addition, we can help by sequestering more rainwater on our properties with rain barrels and rain gardens, which reduces pollution of nearby waterways and allows the water to soak into the soil to replenish the water in the aquifers. I'll cover these topics later in the book.

SPRINGS

There are more than seven hundred springs in Florida, which is the largest collection on the planet! Thirty-three are first-magnitude springs with more than one hundred cubic feet per second (one cubic foot = 7.5 gallons). Eight billion gallons of mostly 72°F water flow from Florida's springs each day. Most of the springs are located in the western areas of the central and northern parts of the state. Fortunately for us, many of the springs are protected and accessible because they're located within local, state, or national parks.

Some of the more notable springs are Ichetucknee Springs, Juniper Springs, Rainbow Springs, Silver Springs, Spring Creek, Three Sisters Springs, Wacissa Spring Group, Wakulla Springs, and Weeki Wachee Springs. Springs are often the sources of water for lakes and rivers.

While it's wonderful that we have access to so many springs, we need to be good citizens as we enjoy them for recreation. We need to be respectful of wildlife, particularly the native West Indian manatees or sea cows (*Trichechus manatus*) that gather at the springs' headwaters to keep warm in the winter. Of course, we don't litter along our waterways, but it's also good to be prepared to pick up any litter or garbage floating in the water or collected along the shorelines. It's up to all of us to keep our springs in the best-possible shape.

One of our favorite adventures is to paddle a mile up the Rainbow River toward its spring, which is located within the Rainbow River State Park. At the boundary of the park, we jump in the water and drift snorkel back downriver towing our kayaks behind us.

Many Florida landscapes include access to bodies of water, and again, we need to be good stewards of the waterways. Our own property backs up to a dammed, spring-fed lake, and there are a series of lakes and ponds in the neighborhood, including a pond in our front yard that we share with a neighbor. It's about a tenth of an acre. Our pond probably does not contain a strong spring, because in years when the dry season is particularly dry, it becomes a mudflat around the edges. During the wet season when it fills up, there is an overflow pipe that empties water into a shallow ravine that runs down to the lake. Living near the water is always interesting.

Swimming with Anhingas in the spring-fed Rainbow River. The Anhinga or snake bird (*Anhinga anhinga*) is a common diving bird in our rivers and lakes.

Lakes

There are thousands of lakes and ponds throughout Florida. Lakes provide important ecosystem services for a wide variety of wildlife, and of course, they also provide recreational opportunities for us. Many of our state parks include lakes of various types so that we may all have access to them. Some of the larger lakes are Dead Lake, Lake Apopka, Lake George, Lake Harney, Lake Istokpoga, Lake Kissimmee, Lake Okeechobee, and Lake Seminole.

Lakes can have low nutrients due to either alkaline or acidic conditions; these typically have crystal clear waters and usually are filled by some of Florida's clear springs. Lakes can also be tea-colored, if they are fed by rivers flowing through acidic, tannin-rich soils, and some lakes are nutrient-rich, filled with lots of vegetation—both floating and emergent.

For many decades, lakes have been focal points for development, which often leads to pollution in the water from lawn-care treatments (synthetic fertilizers, pesticides, and over irrigation), but some developments have better protections built in for the lakes. What people do in their yards matters—because we all live in a watershed. (A watershed is the entire area where rainfall drains into a body of water. No matter where we are, the rain falling on our yard ends up in some body of water, including aquifers.)

Also, as gardeners, it's important to know that lakes and large ponds retain heat or cold and will slow down changes in temperature. They moderate the local weather. For example, Frostproof is a small town in southern Central Florida that is between two good-sized lakes. Farmers there have said their tender crops (mainly citrus) were safer there because of this lake effect.

RIVERS

Rivers serve as the veins forming an interconnected web of the state's water-driven environment. Historically, the rivers have served as transportation corridors and for recreation from fishing to kayaking. Florida has fourteen major rivers, including the Apalachicola River, Caloosahatchee River, Chipola River, Escambia River, Hillsboro Canal, Kissimmee River, Miami Canal, Ochlockonee River, Peace River, Santa Fe River, St. Johns River, St. Marys River, Suwannee River, and Withlacoochee River. Some of those uniquely Floridian names reflect Florida's indigenous peoples, while others reveal the European influence.

Several large rivers in North Florida, including the Ochlockonee, the Apalachicola, and the Suwannee, flow in from other states before emptying into the Gulf of Mexico, which has sometimes caused some interstate arguments over water supply. The St. Johns River is the longest river entirely within Florida, running 310 miles from St. Johns Marsh, which is just west of Vero Beach, northward to Jacksonville, where it takes a sharp eastern turn to empty into the Atlantic Ocean. Along the way, the river drops only thirty feet in elevation, so its flow is quite slow. The slowness, combined with the tidal flows at the mouth of the river, creates a brackish estuary for almost a hundred miles up the river.

Sunrise over the St. Johns River just south of Jacksonville where it's a three-mile-wide estuary with twice daily tidal flows from the Atlantic. It's home to manatees, alligators, Bald Eagles, Ospreys, and much more wildlife.

Estuaries

Estuaries are semienclosed bodies of water, such as bays and lagoons, where freshwater meets and mixes with salty ocean waters. They are dynamic ecosystems with constantly changing tidal flows that cause salinity and water temperatures to fluctuate. Estuaries are sometimes called "the cradles of the ocean," and in Florida, more than 95 percent of our recreationally and commercially important fish, crustaceans, and shellfish spend parts of their lives in estuaries. This is why it's so important to protect them and their water flows from pollution and other harm.

In addition to the mouth of the St. Johns River and the mouths of some other true rivers, we have a variety of estuaries, notably Apalachee Bay, Apalachicola Bay, Biscayne Bay, Charlotte Harbor, Choctawhatchee Bay, Florida Bay, Pensacola Bay, St. Andrews Bay, Tampa Bay, Ten Thousand Islands, and Whitewater Bay. In addition, most stretches of the Florida Intracoastal Waterway, which is located inside a series of barrier islands along the eastern coastline, are also estuaries, even though some are called rivers, lagoons, and lakes. These are created by the frequent breaks between the barrier islands, so they are influenced from the east by tides and storm surges from the Atlantic. They have sources of freshwater from springs and small rivers feeding them from the west. Starting from North Florida, they include the Amelia River, Tolomato River, Matanzas River, Halifax River, Indian River, Banana River, New River, Stranahan River, Indian River Lagoon, and Lake Worth Lagoon.

If your property is near an estuary, you'll need to be aware of the salt exposure to your plants, both from brackish groundwater and from salt spray. You may also wish to learn about living shorelines and oyster reefs, which help improve water quality and provide good habitat for the aquatic ecosystem. To learn more about this, visit the Florida Living Shorelines website, https://floridalivingshorelines.com/.

Florida's Plant Communities

The various hydrological features, as described above, in combination with other factors, including climate, elevation, and soil, have given rise to Florida's unique plant communities, which form the underlying structure of the different ecosystems. According to the Florida Native Plant Society, the different ecosystems can be broadly described as uplands, rocklands, flatlands, grasslands, and wetlands. Each of these is further defined by their locations, soils, water sources, and drainage.

Sandhills and Longleaf Pine Savannas

These xeric (very dry) uplands are found in the central peninsular Florida and up into the Panhandle. These ecosystems are usually fire dependent, and they support quite a few Florida endemic plants—species found only in Florida. Longleaf pine once dominated the coastal plain of the southeastern United States—now only 2 or 3 percent of those forests remain, and most of those remnants are in Florida. I cover more about longleaf pines later.

FLORIDA SCRUB

Another category of xeric uplands are the Florida scrubs—dry, fire-dependent communities that can be found in most of the state. When many people see a scrub area, they think it looks like a wasteland, and as a result, much of Florida's scrub areas have been developed. But our wonderful scrubs are full of unique and endemic plants and animals. Some of these plants are worth the trip. These two photos were taken in Hickory Lake Scrub Park in Polk County. Fortunately, some of Florida's scrubs are now protected in parks and reserves in various parts of Florida.

DRY PRAIRIES

When most people think about Florida's natural areas, *prairie* is probably not a word that comes to mind. But Florida does have prairies: grassland ecosystems where trees and shrubs do not grow for

Feay's palafox (*Palafoxia feayi*) is a woody scrub plant that is native and endemic to Central and South Florida. It's in the aster family, but instead of the typical flower head with disc florets in the center and ray florets around the edge like petals, its flower head has only disc florets, and they are remarkably tubular.

Scrub morning-glory (*Bonamia grandiflora*) is rare and is endemic to Central Florida. The flowers are blue in the morning, but fade to pale lavender during the day.

one reason or another. Unfortunately, most of our dry prairies have been converted to agriculture, but you can understand why—no trees to clear, and no swamp to drain. There are a few remnants preserved in state parks. There are also wet prairies—see below.

Coastal Wetlands

Given Florida's long coastline and its many types of waterways, we have a wide variety of wetland communities. In the tidal areas along the Atlantic and Gulf coasts, we have mangrove forests and salt marshes, which are important for reducing pollution, absorbing storm surges, and protecting against erosion. Since these wetlands are subjected to tides with all their sediments, their soil levels can actually increase in height to keep up with sea-level rise. Also, because these soils lack oxygen, the stored organic matter creates a type of peat that doesn't readily decompose, so this carbon is sequestered much longer than in other soils.

Florida's salt marshes are usually formed in protected areas where the wave action is low. The twice-daily tidal flow and low oxygen levels in the soil limit the diversity of the plants, so these salty wetlands are usually dominated by cordgrasses (*Spartina* spp.) and various rushes and sedges, depending upon the location.

The mangrove forests are so important for the health of shorelines that Florida has passed regulations to govern their management, including trimming and the gathering of propagules. There are three true mangroves native to Florida; all of them tolerate saltwater environments, and all hold on to their seeds until they sprout to form propagules, which can then float away and root quickly once the conditions are favorable:

* Red mangrove (*Rhizophora mangle*). This species grows farthest out in the water. The tangles of prop roots act as stilts and increase stability while also capturing sediments from the surrounding water.
* Black mangrove (*Avicennia germinans*). This species occurs in waters shallower than those of the red mangrove and deeper than those of the white. It grows pneumatophores, strawlike extensions from the roots, to supply oxygen to the roots. This is the most salt tolerant and cold tolerant of the mangroves, so if a mangrove forest is mostly black mangroves, it may indicate that there is a problem with normal tidal flushing and that salts are building up.
* White mangrove (*Laguncularia racemosa*). This species usually occurs on the landward side of the other two and has no obvious root adaptations, but like the others, it handles the salt environment. The leaves look white most of the time because salt is excreted from pores on the leaves.

Buttonwood (*Conocarpus erectus*) is usually included with any discussion of mangroves. It is a small mangrovelike tree or shrub. Buttonwood often grows on the landward side of mangrove ecosystems, but it is not a true mangrove, because its seeds do not sprout while still attached to the parent plant.

Inland Wetlands

There are more than a dozen different types of freshwater wetland plant communities, including basin swamps and marshes, strand swamps, wet prairies, and sloughs.

Wet prairies, especially in the more northern regions of the state, are often characterized by highly acidic soils that offer almost no nutrients to plants. Some plants have adapted to these tough conditions by catching bugs and other small animals to gain the nutrients they need to survive. These carnivorous plants include pitcher plants (*Sarracenia* spp.), sundews (*Drosera* spp.), butterworts (*Pinguicula* spp.), and bladderworts (*Utricularia* spp.). In Florida, wet prairies are more plentiful than dry prairies, and many are preserved in parks and reserves.

A slough (pronounced *slew*) is a shallow, nonforested wetland with slow-moving water. Our largest slough is the Everglades, but there are many smaller sloughs found throughout the state.

The Everglades is a unique subtropical wilderness in South Florida. It consists of 1.5 million acres of sawgrass marshes, mangrove forests, and hardwood hammocks dominated by wetlands. It is home to a wide variety of endangered plants, birds, butterflies, and other wildlife. A portion of it is preserved as a national park.

The water in the Everglades used to flow unimpeded from the headwaters of the Kissimmee River in Central Florida to Lake Okeechobee. Then it flowed southward over low-lying lands. This sixty-mile-wide, slow-moving sheet of water created a mosaic of ponds, marshes, and forests that eventually emptied into Whitewater Bay on the west coast of South Florida. Over thousands of years, this developed into a balanced ecosystem. But in the late 1800s and early 1900s, upon the invention of the rock plow, much of this area was drained and developed mostly for agriculture, especially sugar.

The other name for the Everglades comes from Marjory Stoneman Douglas's seminal book, *The Everglades: River of Grass,* which was first published in 1947. My friend Lucia Robson, who was raised in Florida, gave me a copy when she heard that we were moving here, saying that every new Floridian should know this history. My copy is the fiftieth anniversary edition, which includes an afterword by Douglas, who was ninety-eight years old at the time.

I've briefly described only a few of Florida's remarkable plant communities. A detailed analysis of them all could be another whole book. For more information to our state's native habitats, visit the Florida Native Plant Society website, www.fnps.org/natives/native-plant-communities.

Ecosystems and Gardening

Each of Florida's ecosystems has produced its own suite of plants and animals perfectly adapted to live together within the local conditions. Some plants need wildlife for pollination and for dispersal, while the animals rely on the plants for food and shelter. The local soils and their inhabitants, including millions of microbes, also play a large role in the ecosystem. In Florida, the soil can be quite alkaline if underlain by limestone, but in other areas, the soils can be clayey or sandy, both of which are usually slightly acidic.

It's a useful exercise for us, as gardeners, to determine what plant community might have been in place before our neighborhoods were developed. While we plant our yards for today's conditions, our choices for plants and landscaping should be influenced by our knowledge of what grew here before development. That way, we can better support the birds and the pollinators that evolved within the local habitat. Probably the best way to do this is to visit parks and preserves closest to your house to learn what the land and the local ecosystems may have been like and to see what native plants are growing there.

Not all native plants local to your area will work well in typical suburban yards, but there will be some that are recommended and that are found in the native plant trade. The Florida Native Plant Society maintains a sizable list of recommended native plants, and you can create a list of specific types of plants that are native to your county. More on this later.

Florida's Planting Zones

Florida's climate includes eight USDA plant hardiness zones (8a, 8b, 9a, 9b, 10a, 10b, 11a, and 11b), so Florida has a wide range of climates and conditions. When Dean and I arrived in 2004, the old 1990 planting

The 2012 U.S. Department of Agriculture. Plant Hardiness Zone Map, is the most-recent version as of this printing. Accessed from https://planthardiness.ars.usda.gov/.

zone map indicated that our house in Clay County was on the line between zones 8b and 9a. I used to joke that our master bedroom area was in a cooler zone. The 2012 map moved that line up to the Florida-Georgia border—about an hour's drive north. Now we're solidly in zone 9a with average low temperatures between 20 and 25°F.

The average low temperature has long been used to guide gardeners in the timing of planting projects, and the map has been on seed packets for as long as I can remember. But in addition to these broad patterns, there are other considerations, too: microclimates caused by moisture, shade, and retained heat of rocks or cement infrastructure; prevailing on-shore breezes; and more.

Also, in Florida, high temperatures can limit what and when we can grow stuff. I already discussed the warm periods during winter limiting our ability to grow tulips and other plants that need a sustained cold period during the winter. In the summer, the average nighttime low temperatures are higher than 73°F, which means that most tomatoes won't set fruit in the summer. I'll discuss this later, but all this demonstrates that knowing the average low temperatures is only one part of the picture.

Florida's Light

The light a garden bed receives varies from season to season. There are two main factors in how light in the winter differs from light in the summer. First, of course, is the number of hours of daylight each day—fewer in winter and more in summer.

The second major difference between light in summer and winter is the intensity. The sun stays lower in the sky during winter. This is because Florida is in the northern hemisphere, and the Earth is tilted away from the sun, which causes its light to be weaker and less intense as it passes through more of the atmosphere from that angle. The shorter hours of daylight and the weaker sunlight are what cause our weather to become cooler during winter. Compared to much of the United States, however, Florida's wintertime reduction of light intensity is somewhat less pronounced, since Florida (especially South Florida) is closer to the tropics. The Tropic of Cancer is only about seventy miles south of Key West.

The other effect of the lower angle involves shadows. Objects cast longer shadows in winter than in summer. A bed that gets direct sun most of the day in summer may be totally shaded by longer shadows in winter. Also, when deciduous trees drop their leaves, normally shady areas become somewhat sunnier. Knowing a plant's light needs should be factored into planting decisions. This can increase the success rate for our plants and our gardens.

Florida's Rainfall

Florida's rainfall is uneven throughout the year, and in most areas of the state, 60 to 70 percent of the annual rainfall is in the five-month wet season (that is, the hurricane season) from June through October.

So even though Florida's annual rainfall averages about fifty inches, those seven dry months can be almost arid, with only an inch of rain or less each month. In other words, in most of the state, most of the time, Florida receives too much or too little rain for perfect growing conditions. The rainfall in the Florida Panhandle is a bit more even throughout the year, but the whole state is different from the more temperate climates to the north, where the rain is more evenly spaced throughout the year. For instance, New York City receives three or four inches of rainfall each month, on average.

Our hot, wet summers can be another limiting factor in the garden. Most members of the squash family are subject to fungal blights, and so are other crops like tomatoes and basil. There are notable exceptions, such as the Seminole pumpkin (*Cucurbita moschata*), which thrives in our hot, wet summers. This plant is native to Mexico, but it was traded by the various indigenous peoples and was being grown in Florida when the Europeans first arrived five hundred years ago. I'll discuss this interesting crop later.

Florida Is Unique

Florida's climate, hydrological features, and varied ecosystems make our state different from the rest of the country. Even gardeners with years of experience, like me, have had to relearn when and what we can and cannot grow here. Of course, our native plants are perfectly suited to our climate, which brings us to the next topic . . .

2

❧

Understanding the "Real Florida"

More than five hundred years ago when the Spanish explorer Ponce de León landed in Florida near today's St. Augustine, one legend says that he thought the land, with its magnificent flowers, was so beautiful that he named it La Florida—land of the flowers. Nonetheless, European settlers and missionaries brought many plants from their home countries, which transformed much of Florida to look more like European landscapes and less like what people call "the Real Florida." I must confess that I also started out doing the same thing. Even after my failure in planting tulips, I looked for plants that would survive in Florida such as calla lilies, hurricane lilies, and more. But when I joined the Florida Native Plant Society in 2006, my thinking shifted from what *could* grow here to what belongs here. I had begun to appreciate the Real Florida.

This seems so obvious, and you'd think that building a native Florida yard should be easy. But no. There are various entrenched traditions such as formal, showy seasonal plantings of mostly non-native plants and practices such as "instant" landscaping, where experts come in and do a complete planting all at once, implying that landscaping is an event, not an ongoing process. A whole group of businesses have been built around catering to these unrealistic and unsustainable gardening ideals. These gardening ideals started hundreds of years ago with the extensive formal gardens and expansive lawns surrounding the mansions of upper-class people in Europe and the British Isles. These formal landscapes were status symbols demonstrating how wealthy they were, because it took so many gardeners to keep them in shape, and back then, it was expensive to import non-native plants from around the world.

The ideal of formal landscapes has been pushed onto gardeners in this country by gardening magazines, landscape contests, and more recently, TV shows and social media. Often there are "before and after" photos and videos, which imply that once the "after" landscapes are installed, they are done: *Voilà*! The truth is that landscapes are never "done," because plants are not static decoration items. While some will grow to be just perfect for their locations, others will die for no apparent reason, and still others will become too exuberant. Then there are the unwanted volunteer plants—the wrong plants in the wrong places—that need to be pulled. So there is no such thing as an instant landscape: landscaping is not an event—it's an ongoing process.

Local garden centers cater to the formal garden ideal by offering masses of pretty annuals, such as marigolds, petunias, pansies, begonias, and impatiens, in full bloom. As a botanist, I can tell you that these plants have nearly completed their mission in life to germinate, grow, produce flowers, and set seed. When you plant them in your yard, they'll be on their downhill slide, and most will probably last only a few months. This works well for the garden centers, because each season you'll be back to buy the next set of pretty plants. They are generally not very expensive, but when you add the cost for replacing these plants two or three times a year, year after year, they are *not* inexpensive—either for your family budget or for the work involved.

The behind-the-scenes business partners in this mix are the commercial growers of these pretty-on-the-shelf annuals that supply the garden centers. Their goal is to produce clean, bug-free flowers quickly and cheaply. To accomplish this, the growers sometimes use systemic insecticides, usually neonicotinoids that are absorbed into every part of the plant. These poisons kill any bug that eats the plant. The problem with these plants in our gardens is that the systemic poisons remain in the plant tissues, so these plants will kill the pollinators, the butterfly larvae, the beneficial insects, and more. They defeat the very purpose of butterfly gardens. Each treated plant is supposed to be labeled, so pay attention, because they are the *last* thing you want in

Non-native annuals in full bloom offer gardeners instant gratification, but in the long run they are not sustainable. Because they are replaced so often, they are expensive, require a lot of labor, and the repeated soil disturbances disrupt soil ecosystems and release more CO_2 into the air.

your butterfly garden. (See chapter 4 for details on building effective pollinator gardens.)

(Note: In this book, with apologies to the entomologists, I'll be using the term "bug" in the general sense to include all insects, plus spiders, mites, and other creepy-crawly organisms, not just the order of insects known as "true bugs"—the sucking insects such as aphids.)

As a result of Floridians using mostly non-native plants in their yards and in their communities, our landscapes are filled with impatiens native to Africa, begonias and crepe myrtles native to India, pansies from Europe, petunias and philodendrons native to South America, azaleas and figs from Asia, and more. These landscapes could be anywhere in the world. They do not look like Florida, and they have not coevolved with Florida's fauna, which means that they don't usually play vital roles in the local ecosystems to support the pollinators and the birds.

A more serious consequence of importing all these non-native plants is that some of them have escaped cultivation, and some have become invasive in Florida. A plant is determined to be invasive only after it's degraded or replaced large areas of Florida's natural ecosystems.

The official list of invasive plants in our state is kept up-to-date by the Florida Invasive Species Council (FISC; https://floridainvasivespecies. org). This organization maintains a list of invasive plants with two categories: Category I, where the plants have already done significant damage, and Category II, where the plants have done some damage and could do more. There are about seventy-five plants in each category. This list also indicates whether a plant is invasive in North, Central, or South Florida.

Controlling invasive plants in Florida's natural areas and waterways is expensive, costing taxpayers and environmental organizations millions of dollars each year. Yet at this point, many invasives are still for sale in garden centers. To help Florida's natural spaces, it's a good idea to spend a little time figuring out what is invasive in your region; then, don't buy them, and work to remove those that are already on your property and in your community. Many are tenacious and will come back after the initial removal from roots or seeds left in the soil, but keep at it. This process will become easier if you help your neighbors take the same steps. That way, there will be fewer seeds from nearby yards, which will reduce the spread for everyone. Be part of the solution.

All of this brings us back to appreciating the Real Florida as a more sustainable alternative to those seasonal plantings of non-natives. But first of all, why are native plants important?

Why Natives?

Native plants are those that occur naturally in a region and form the ecological basis upon which life depends, including birds, pollinators, and other native wildlife adapted to that ecosystem. Without the native plants and the insects that coevolved with them, the plants will not be pollinated as effectively and local birds may have more difficulty surviving. Native plant enthusiasts have been preaching this narrative for decades, but in 2007, entomology professor Douglas W. Tallamy changed the narrative with the release of his compelling book, *Bringing Nature Home: How You Can Sustain Wildlife with Native Plants.* His research in Delaware showed that native oak trees (*Quercus* spp.)

Invasive Plants

Invasive and *aggressive* are not interchangeable terms when describing exuberant plants. There are plenty of aggressive plants that are native to Florida. A good example is Spanish needles (*Bidens alba*), which will happily take over any bare soil—it's an effective pioneer plant. I've pulled out bushels of them when they've crowded out my vegetable crops or planted themselves in areas where I was trying to establish other natives. But I always leave a stand in the back corners and in meadow areas, because so many pollinators love them. So Spanish needles are certainly aggressive, but not invasive, since they are native and they belong in Florida's ecosystems. The term *invasive* is only used for the non-native plants on the Florida Invasive Species Council's Category I and Category II lists. For more information, see https://floridainvasivespecies.org/.

Spanish needles (*Bidens alba*) is an aggressive Florida native. It's visited by a wide variety of pollinators, including the polka-dotted waspmoth (*Syntomeida epilais*) (pictured). This is an unusual day-flying moth with bright coloration to warn birds that these moths are toxic. The larvae feed on poisonous plants in the dogbane family—mostly oleanders these days.

support more than five hundred species of caterpillars, whereas ginkgo (*Ginkgo biloba*), a widely planted urban tree native to China, hosts only five. He also estimated that it takes between six thousand and nine thousand caterpillars for a pair of chickadees to raise a clutch of babies from hatching to fledging. Caterpillars are slow-moving prey, so they are easy to catch; also, they are full of fat and protein, and without a hard exoskeleton, they are easier to digest than other bugs. Ninety-six percent of North American terrestrial birds feed caterpillars to their young.

The most common advice to create a bird-friendly yard is to plant a wide variety of native plants with seeds and berries ripening throughout the year. While this holds true for adult birds because seeds and berries provide nutritious food for birds, especially in the winter, it's the insects that are more important for feeding growing fledglings. I can summarize this in one sentence: If you want to invite birds to your yard, you first have to invite the bugs. The first step in this task is to stop all landscape-wide pesticides, including lawn-care applications— no insecticides, no herbicides, and no fungicides. I cover this in more detail in the chapter about lawns.

Native Plants Attract Bugs, Which Attract Birds

In contrast to those seasonal plantings, a native landscape is usually designed for the long term, so the plants tend to be perennials and self-seeding annuals in addition to groupings of shrubs and trees. The initial cost of the plants is usually more than those seasonal annuals, but these plants are allowed to live out their full life cycles, so in the end, your monetary investment will probably be less.

Another advantage of not digging up the plants two or three times each year is that soil ecosystems in these beds can stabilize after the initial planting. Recent studies have found that the rhizosphere (the area around plants' roots) is a complex and dynamic region with various chemicals released by the plant root and the surrounding soil microorganisms. Bacteria and fungi in the soil, especially mycorrhizal fungi, help plants absorb more water and more nutrients. Healthy soils can better support the plants. In other words, if you take care of the soil by not drenching it with pesticides and synthetic fertilizers and not digging it up several times a year, the soil will take care of your plants. I cover soil and soil ecosystems in more detail in chapter 7.

Native plantings can take many forms depending upon your landscape, but most often, the designs tend to replicate natural ecosystems. For a border area, you might use a combination of bunching grasses and a variety of perennials so that something is in bloom all year. I provide more details on building native habitat in your yard in chapters 3 and 4.

Also, keep in mind that Florida is a large state, so just because a plant is native to Florida that doesn't mean that it's native to the whole state. For instance, the purple coneflower (*Echinacea purpurea*), a favorite pollinator plant, is native to most of the eastern United States from Texas northward to Wisconsin, eastward to New York, and southward to only one small county in Florida's Panhandle in planting zone 8a. While you could attempt to grow it in other parts of Florida, it will probably grow only as an annual instead of a perennial because it needs more consistent cold in the winter than most of Florida can provide. Part of our education as Florida gardeners is knowing which plants are native to our own counties. Read on.

Where to Find Native Plants

If the typical garden centers and the garden sections of the big box stores offer mostly non-native plants, what are your options? Fortunately, here in Florida, there are several organizations working to make natives the new normal.

First, there's the Florida Native Plant Society (FNPS), with more than thirty chapters around the state. The chapters are your local, feet-on-the-ground native plant enthusiasts. The chapters hold educational meetings, host field trips, and participate in outreach events; most chapters hold or coordinate local native plant sales. The state FNPS organization organizes an annual conference with multiple presentations, a multivendor plant sale, and field trips.

The FNPS website (www.fnps.org/plants) includes an important application where you can generate a list of various categories of recommended plants such as shrubs or butterfly plants that are native to your county. Each plant profile includes planting information, several photos, and more, plus a link to native nurseries that have it in stock. (Full disclosure: 50 percent of the royalties for this book will be paid directly to FNPS. I'm an enthusiastic supporter of this nonprofit organization.)

The Florida Association of Native Nurseries (FANN) is an organization of native nurseries and native landscapers. If you're serious about building a Florida native yard, having a working relationship with your local native nursery will make this easier to accomplish. You can search for a specific plant or for a local native nursery on their website, www.plantrealflorida.org.

The Florida Wildflowers Growers Cooperative offers seeds for our most popular wildflowers. The best time to plant many of them is in the fall; visit them at www.floridawildflowers.com.

Ready; Set; Go Native!

I shared my adventures in transforming our yard in my Transplanted Gardener columns because I thought that gardeners would appreciate the less-managed landscape filled with plants native to the region, which supports our native wildlife. While I wrote a number of columns on this topic over the years, the one that best demonstrates the overall transformation to an effective habitat for wildlife was the one I wrote on how we certified our yard.

Creating Backyard Habitat

We began working on various projects to make our property more attractive to wildlife and to increase its environmental sustainability as soon as we moved here in 2004. I wrote about many of these projects, including rain gardens, rain barrels, native plants in our landscape, reducing our lawn, creating and maintaining meadow areas, and more. My columns were a type of journal so readers could see that native landscaping is a process.

Two years after we moved here, I decided it was time to apply to become a Certified Wildlife Habitat certification from the National Wildlife Federation (NWF). Our yard became NWF habitat 59063. I urge everyone to do this. It's not difficult, and if you have children at home, certification is an interesting and educational family project. In 2021, NWF has recognized over 250,000 Certified Wildlife Habitat gardens in the United States, including backyards, urban gardens, school grounds, businesses, places of worship, campuses, parks, farms, zoos, and community landscapes.

Four Features for Wildlife Habitat

Food. You need to provide a minimum of three types of food: seeds, berries, leaves, nuts, nectar, and pollen. Food is best supplied by native plants and animals in a balanced ecosystem. Many people supplement the naturally occurring food with feeders, but this may cause an imbalance in wildlife populations. For instance, pigeons are rarely attracted to suburban yards unless there are bird feeders.

Water. You need to provide at least one source of water for drinking and bathing. We have a pond in the front of our house and a 110-acre lake is at the back of our lot, so we qualified. If you don't have a pond, you could create a small water feature with a solar pump, to keep the water flowing and cooler than a static birdbath. Or you could just have a birdbath in the shade and change the water daily.

Cover. Wildlife habitat requires places where wildlife can find shelter from weather and predators. You need to provide two areas with cover. Good cover includes places where animals can hide while active but also when in dormant stages. It can be provided by native trees, shrubs, brambles, and brush piles. It's important that the cover be regionally appropriate to best support the local birds and pollinators. Our lot includes a number of these features, but you don't need a big space to provide cover.

Places to raise young. While much of the cover and food features above double for this category, the emphasis is different. This category also includes nesting sites such as meadows, mature trees, and dead trees or snags, plus food for larvae and other young.

Sustainable Gardening

In addition to the four habitat features, NWF requires that you practice at least two sustainable gardening practices such as installing rain gardens, mulching and composting, reducing lawn areas, reducing erosion, reducing chemicals, and more. We'd been working from the beginning to minimize environmentally negative conditions and to also reduce maintenance for our property.

In hindsight, I think this exercise was the initial inspiration for my first book, *Sustainable Gardening for Florida.* When I met an editor for the University Press of Florida at a writers' conference, he asked if I could write an organic gardening book for Florida, I said, "Sure." But in my proposal for that first book, my pitch was how sustainable gardening is more important and would be of interest to a broader audience. Ironically, my next book was the book he was looking for: *Organic Methods for Vegetable Gardening in Florida,* with Melissa Contreras in Miami as my coauthor. I met her on my first Florida book tour when she was coordinating events at Fairchild Tropical Botanic Garden.

Create a Plant List

I had been paying attention and had identified most of the larger plants in our yard, but this exercise inspired me to expand my plant list in an organized manner. The plant list on our property included more than a hundred species, including the several invasive species that I worked to eradicate (and even today, some of them keep coming back because they are still in our neighbors' yards). If you need help in identifying plants, see the resources below.

It was a great feeling to get the NWF package in the mail and to hang the sign on an oak tree at the front corner of the yard. Now all these years later, the sign is a bit faded, but it serves as a bit of outreach to my neighbors to let them know that what we have been doing in our yard is on purpose.

Maintenance of Native Landscapes

People assume that natives will be much easier to care for because they belong in the local ecosystem. To a large extent this is true, but your yard is not a natural ecosystem, and the influence of the gardener is evident. Native landscapes usually require at least some regular maintenance, especially in urban and suburban neighborhoods, where the appearance of looking cared for is the expectation. When compared to the default landscape of more formal gardens, where the plants are replaced as soon as they get a bit leggy, your non-dead-headed natives may be perceived as unruly. And your native meadow area—filled with bunching grasses and pollinator plants that are allowed to go to seed, so the birds have seeds to eat over the winter—might look like a bunch of weeds to your neighbors.

The best strategy in neighborhoods where neatness matters is to make the edges of the meadows more civilized by installing a border of bunching grasses or small shrubs. Another strategy is to mow a gently curving path through the meadow that might lead to a bench under a shade tree. These actions, much like our certified habitat sign, indicate that this is a cared-for landscape and is wild with a purpose.

One of the most visible changes we made to our landscape was to stop mowing an area out front that the previous owner had sodded. It was more than a tenth of an acre that was surrounded by mature trees. We maintained it as a meadow by weed whacking it once a year in the winter and by digging out the volunteer trees before they grew too large. We kept it as a meadow for five or six years, but then we missed the winter maintenance for a couple of years. The trees grew, and this area became a woods. Keep this in mind as you work on your yard: the landscaping may evolve as the plants grow or as your needs change.

Florida-Friendly Landscaping

And speaking of neighbors and maintenance, Florida Yards and Neighborhoods is a homeowner-focused program of the University of Florida/IFAS Extension Service and the Florida Department of Environmental Protection, in cooperation with the five Water

Management Districts. Under the Florida Yards and Neighborhoods umbrella, UF/IFAS Extension has organized the Florida-Friendly Landscaping program, where you can participate in workshops or classes and get your yard certified as a Florida-Friendly Landscape. While it represents a potentially big improvement in making home landscapes more environmentally friendly, and the sponsoring organizations have spent a lot of time and energy on outreach to shift people from perfect lawns and perfect gardens trimmed to a fare-thee-well, I do have a couple of problems with this program. First, only about half of the recommended "Florida-Friendly" plants are Florida natives; second, turfgrass management is only slightly modified, to reduce runoff. As you'll see in the next chapter, I promote freedom lawns with no synthetic fertilizers.

The nine principles of Florida-Friendly Landscaping are (1) planting the right plant in the right place, (2) watering efficiently, (3) fertilizing appropriately, (4) mulching, (5) attracting wildlife, (6) managing yard pests responsibly, (7) recycling yard waste, (8) reducing stormwater runoff, and (9) protecting the waterfront. For more information on the Florida-Friendly Landscaping program, see https://ffl.ifas.ufl.edu/.

In 2012, Florida instituted a Florida-friendly landscaping law, which states that yards that are designed with the following nine governing principles are allowed, even if there are homeowners' association (HOA) rules on landscaping. To read the official wording of the law, see www.flsenate.gov/Laws/Statutes/2012/373.185.

Most native yards would be considered to be Florida-friendly because they attract wildlife and more. I'll cover some of these principles further in this book. Be sure to consult your deed restrictions, your HOA, and/or your Architectural Review Committee before making significant landscape changes. This is not legal advice, and such laws are subject to interpretation; keep in mind that a sharp HOA lawyer may find ways to circumvent the intent of the Florida-friendly landscaping statute.

What Is Beautiful?

There is a movement to change the perception of what a beautiful garden should look like. Some prominent public gardens have gone

The popular High Line park in New York City is planted with mostly natives that are not dead-headed, so the birds are attracted to this park even in the dense urban area of western Manhattan. Public gardens like this that are filled with natives are changing the perception of what beautiful gardens are supposed to look like.

native. Their plants are allowed to grow to their own shapes and go to seed to feed the birds. The High Line park in New York City and the Lurie Garden in Chicago are two famous examples, but there are many more.

We can continue this trend in Florida with our native yards and by working within our communities to overcome those long-held beliefs that formal gardens and acres of unused lawn are ideal landscapes. Of course, we can set an example with our own yards, but speaking up at meetings and hearings can make all the difference. To make it easier for you to speak out, Marjorie Shropshire and I put together a free, downloadable PowerPoint presentation for you to use. We included a script, which is about ten minutes long, if read along with the slides. It's available on the Florida Native Plant Society website, under resources and downloadable documents, https://www.fnps.org/resources/pubs. It's a Gardening with Natives document titled "Why Native Landscapes Are Important"; it downloads as a PDF file, but the link to the presentation itself is in that file.

As we convert our yards and public community spaces, including schools, churches, business properties, municipal properties, and other general community lands, more and more people will realize that Ponce de León was right all those years ago: that the Real Florida is indeed beautiful, and that it lives up to its given name—land of the flowers.

Resources

A complete online reference for Florida plants is the Atlas of Florida Plants, which is maintained by the Institute for Systematic Botany at the University of South Florida. It includes all of our native plants and those non-natives that have escaped cultivation. It is the authority on whether or not a plant species is native. For each species profile, it provides a map with the plant range, and most profiles include several photos; find it at https://florida.plantatlas.usf.edu/.

The Florida Wildflower Foundation has good information on its website on various plants and their pollinators. The organization also has several important initiatives including hosting webinars, roadside wildflower projects, and grants to schools, nature centers, botanical gardens, and city, county, and state parks to establish native wildflower plantings; visit them at https://flawildflowers.org.

The Institute for Regional Conservation (IRC) provides a detailed plant database for South Florida by zip code; this organization is dedicated to the protection, restoration, and long-term management of biodiversity on a regional basis. It provides information in Spanish as well; see www.regionalconservation.org.

The National Wildlife Federation has been spearheading its backyard and schoolyard habitat certification since 1973; their site is at www.nwf.org.

Audubon's website provides descriptions, plans, guidelines, and kids' activities for creating and maintaining bird-friendly backyards; see www.audubon.org/native-plants.

3

~

Lawns in Florida

Much like the formal gardens, the all-American lawn is a centuries-old leftover from British and European nobility when a large lawn indicated wealth. Lawns didn't gain popularity in this country until the early 1900s, when the Garden Club of America set the standard with their annual contests for the best-looking yards. At that time, there were push lawn mowers and garden hoses to make the maintenance manageable. Before then, if you wanted a lawn, you'd need grazing animals to keep the grass at a more or less even height. Woodrow Wilson had a herd of sheep keeping the White House lawn trimmed and fertilized. Americans' real love affair with lawns began after World War II, when developments were built to house families of returning soldiers and where each household had a small lawn that was mowed with a hand-pushed lawn mower. Upon the invention of gas-powered mowers, the lawns grew larger and larger.

Roughly 30 percent of the water used in urban and suburban areas in the eastern states goes to landscape irrigation, mostly lawns. And in this century, the lawn acreage around the country is so vast that it is the largest irrigated crop in the country, having five times the acreage of corn, the second largest crop. In Florida alone, there are more than four million acres of lawn, and while this number includes golf courses, a significant portion of this total is homeowners' lawns.

In these days of extended droughts and water restrictions, rethinking our lawns makes good sense for many reasons.

Lawns in Florida

The default landscape in Florida's developments and neighborhoods is often a highly managed lawn with a fringe of shrubs around the foundation and maybe a lone tree or two plunked in the middle of the lawn.

Because it's not easy to maintain a monoculture of turfgrass in Florida, where pest insects can attack and weeds can intrude in a blink of an eye, most Florida homeowners hire lawn-care companies to do the work. Lawn-care companies routinely apply landscape-wide pesticides, including insecticides, fungicides, and herbicides, and since those chemicals are not good for grass or for the soil ecosystem, they then apply synthetic fertilizers to keep the grass alive. Also in the winter, when lawns would normally go dormant in Florida, they often overseed the whole lawn with annual ryegrass (*Lolium multiflorum*), so the lawn stays unnaturally green, and so the lawn guys will have something to mow throughout the winter—a type of job security.

With continued applications, the soil becomes more inert; eventually, it serves only as an anchor for the turfgrass instead of a supportive growing medium. And the treatments for the lawn will continue to weaken its web of support for sustaining life. When the turf finally dies, the homeowners are often required to replace the whole lawn with new sod to start the process all over again. Isn't this the definition of insanity? Doing the same thing over and over, and each time expecting that the results will be different.

In addition, there have been significant, destructive environmental consequences due to lawn chemicals. They wash from our landscapes and pollute our waterways with too many nutrients, turning them green with slime or causing toxic red tides as algae reacts to all those nutrients. They also pollute our aquifers, which is the source for 90 percent of our drinking water. In several areas in the state, there are fertilizer bans throughout the wet season and year-round regulations disallowing synthetic fertilizers with phosphorus. Thus people are limited to fertilizers marked with NPK (nitrogen-phosphorus-potassium) numbers such as "16-0-8" or "15-0-15." You should know that while these synthetic fertilizers provide a quick boost for the turf growth in the short term, in the long run, they overstimulate and harm the soil ecosystem, and they readily wash through the soil into the stormwater systems.

In addition, the landscape-wide insecticide applications kill our native bees and other beneficial insects and destroy their habitat, which is mostly in the ground. The lawn care companies install little signs advising that, for three to five days after application, you, your kids, and your pets are not to walk on the lawn. This means that they admit that these poisons are not good for us or our pets.

You can do as we did, and just say no.

When we first moved into our house, the lawn-care guys who had worked for the former owner stopped by to offer to continue their services. When I refused, they said that without their pesticides (fungicides, insecticides, and herbicides) and their specially formulated fertilizer and weed-and-feed applications, our lawn would die. Well, as it turns out, a few months later some brown spots did develop, but they were soon taken over by other plants, which those lawn guys would probably have condemned as "weeds."

Over the years, the diversity of our lawn has increased dramatically and now there are more than a hundred species of plants, including a fair proportion of the St. Augustine grass (*Stenotaphrum secundatum*) left over from the former owners' sodded lawn. Later, I learned that the term for our mow-what's-there lawn is "freedom lawn," which is a mowed area that is free from all landscape-wide pesticide applications, free from synthetic fertilizers, free from overseeding, and free from overirrigation. Most of the time our freedom lawn looks just as green as our neighbors' expensive, high-maintenance lawns.

We are fortunate that our neighborhood includes wooded lots with a reasonable diversity of mature trees that support abundant bird populations, so seeds in the ground are abundant: it's our seed bank. If you live in a newer development away from wooded areas and where the soil may be more sterile, the diversity increase will probably be slower. There are ways to hurry the process, such as planting native ground covers in bare spots.

If you live in a community with homeowners' association (HOA)

Our freedom lawn after five years without lawn-care poisons or fertilizers. Note: The path and shrubs in the foreground replaced a section of shaded lawn that wasn't doing well.

A closer look at our lawn shows some of the wide variety of plants in our freedom lawn.

regulations dealing with lawns, I'm not going to provide legal advice, but I suggest treading softly and working with your board before you begin doing anything major with your landscape, so they know what your plans are. Even though the Florida-friendly statute may legally overrule these regulations, you probably don't want a fight. What HOAs are trying to accomplish is to have a neighborhood that is well cared for. When your landscape looks presentable and neat, then that should help change some minds. I know people who have reduced their lawns little by little, so the neighbors hardly noticed the changes.

Freedom Lawn Conversion Strategies

If you inherited a highly poisoned, overfertilized, and overirrigated lawn, it's likely that the roots of the turfgrass are short and weak. This is due to the frequent close-cropped mowings, the frequent pesticide and synthetic fertilizer applications, and the frequent irrigation. The turf will have become highly dependent on that intense lawn care because those treatments will have impaired the underlying soil's ecosystem. The soil in these cases serves only to anchor the turf in place.

The best strategy, after stopping all the pesticide and synthetic fertilizer applications, is to ease the strain on the grass. Here are several ways to move to more sustainable care.

Mow less often and set the blade on your mower to the highest setting (usually four or five inches). This extra leaf area (where photosynthesis takes place) allows the grass to create more sugars for itself. The longer grass also shades the soil, which helps the soil hold its moisture and reduces the heat fluctuations. Don't bag or rake the clippings—leave them in place to serve as a mulch and to add natural nutrients to the soil. Do spread out or remove big clumps of clippings so the grass and other plants are not smothered. I rake up the big clumps of mowed lawn and use them in my compost pile. (More on mowing strategies below.)

Gradually shift the irrigation so that you water deeply once a week, but only when needed. This encourages deep roots. (See below for more on irrigation.)

Even after years of poison applications, a soil ecosystem will begin to recover by itself as soon as the pesticide and fertilizer applications are stopped. You can hurry the recovery. For the first year or two, in early spring, well outside our five wet-season months, apply a thin layer (about a quarter of an inch) of compost on the lawn and gently water it in. The compost offers some nutrients to the soil, but unlike synthetic fertilizers, the compost—with its millions of microbes—will become part of the soil and will help repair the soil ecosystem. The compost will also add humus to the soil, so it can retain the moisture for much longer. Healthy soil can better support the plants. Also, this natural, light amount of fertilization means that the grass will grow slower than when it is fed with multiple synthetic fertilizer applications during the year. And ending where we began: This less-fertilized lawn won't need to be mowed as often.

Reducing the Lawn

There are two main methods that we've used to reduce our lawn acreage over the years. One method we used was to just stop mowing, as we did with our whole front area, mentioned earlier, which we maintained as a meadow area. The second method has been to actually remove lawn, especially around the edges. Our lawn area is now about half of what it was when we moved in, and the new edges have been designed with gentle curves and no vertical edges. This way, the mowing is easier and no follow-up trimming is needed.

Stop Mowing

Just letting the grass grow is certainly the easiest way to get a start on a meadow, but in densely populated neighborhoods, there may be a perception that you're not caring for your yard. So it's probably best to use this strategy in the backyard or other areas that won't be so visible. An alternative is to create a tidier border of small shrubs or bunching grasses and to plant groupings of meadow wildflowers scattered through the unmowed area. Choose several types of wildflowers so that something is always in bloom. Adding a sign, like we did, saying

Two areas where we simply let the grass grow: One was this shady triangle with one point being a tree we lost in the 2004 hurricanes. The second area is in the distance, on top of the septic system drain field mound, where we must not allow any trees or large rooted plants to grow. It's mowed once or twice a year, and we dig out trees that survive this treatment.

that this is a native landscape will help improve the perception that it's not just an overgrown lawn.

Another issue with just letting the turfgrass grow is that it will probably set seed and increase its own population where you are looking for greater diversity. In one area, out back where we had just let the grass grow and where, later, I'd planted some trees and shrubs at the edge of a wooded area, I eventually ripped out all the St. Augustine grass because it's not what I wanted there. I had to repeat the exercise the next two years because the remnants had regrown. I wanted the ferns and the native ground covers to dominate that shady area—not grass. So when you take this road to less lawn, work to visualize what you are trying to accomplish, because it may be easier to completely remove the grass at the start.

KILLING OR REMOVING LAWN

There are several ways to kill or remove lawn.

Use a broad-spectrum herbicide. Apply to the area and wait the prescribed number of days before sowing seeds or installing plants. As previously noted, the use of herbicides is not generally recommended for routine lawn care, but it's probably the most effective method for killing off the whole lawn, especially if you have a lot of deep-rooted weeds. Carefully follow directions for use. Do not use herbicides anywhere close to trees or shrubs and certainly do not use them on windy days. This is the method that's often used for the roadside meadow programs.

Kill the turf by covering it with layers of newspaper or cardboard covered with mulch. The mulch could be chipped wood from local tree cutters, topsoil, compost, or dead leaves. Irrigate the area so the mulch doesn't blow away and to start the decay of the paper. Install plants into the mulch and cut into the paper so roots can easily access the soil below. An alternative to this is to use large leaves like palm fronds, banana leaves, or elephant ear leaves instead of paper.

Kill the grass with a layer of mulch or dead leaves without the paper. Without the paper, the mulch needs to be thick enough so no light gets to the soil—six or eight inches usually works. You may need to rake some of the mulch aside when you're ready to install your plants. (I discuss more on mulching in chapter 7.)

Solarize. Cover an area with clear plastic sheets that are well anchored around the edges. Leave these in place for five or six weeks— summer is the best time to do this. This kills not only the grass, but also the weed seeds, root-knot nematodes, and other soil critters. In addition, solarization can melt drip irrigation equipment, so remove that before you start. An in-ground computerized irrigation system is deep enough, so it will be fine, but do remove any sprinkler heads at the surface. Temporarily cap the pipe at its below-ground junction.

Dig or rake the turf. You can remove it by hand or rent a sod cutter for larger areas. This is the most labor-intensive method, but it may be the quickest in the long run. Use the removed turf (but not the noxious weeds) in your compost pile. You could also remove the turf as large chunks of sod to fill in dead spots in the lawn areas you wish to keep.

I have used the hand-removal method for many of my lawn-removal projects over the years, but I try to minimize the soil disruption. In addition, since St. Augustine grass has runners, I pull them out away from the new edge of the lawn and bend them back into the lawn, tucking them under other runners. This minimizes the regrowth at the edge. If you cut off the runners right at the edge, the plant hormones will cause two new sprouts at each cut. Some other turfgrasses commonly used in Florida, such as centipedegrass (*Eremochloa ophiuroides*), also have runners, but others do not. You will have to adjust to your situation.

Then I mulch those new edges of the lawn with leaves, wood chips, or pine needles to reduce new weeds. I normally make a run around the edges every couple of years—not all at once, but section by section as I get to it between other chores and traveling. With each round of lawn edge reduction, there is less for Dean to mow.

Okay, Where to Start?

If you're beginning lawn reduction in your new Florida landscape, removing lawn from around trees and wooded areas is probably the best place to start. Trees and lawns are not good neighbors for several reasons.

Trees and shrubs have much more leaf surface area than mowed grass. This means that their transpiration rate is much higher. (Transpiration is the process of water being absorbed by the roots, pulled up through the xylem tubes, and evaporating into the air through the stomata, or leaf pores.) So in the contest for water from the soil, the trees will always win.

Most trees have shallow, wide-spreading roots that increase in girth each year and many tend to emerge above the soil and eventually interfere with mowing. This is a more serious problem for some trees, such as maples (*Acer* spp.) and sweetgums (*Liquidambar styraciflua*).

Both evergreen and deciduous trees lose their leaves or needles at some time during the year. Some trees, such as our southern magnolia

(*Magnolia grandiflora*), lose their leaves all year long. These leaves or needles tend to smother the turfgrass if not raked away, but if they fall into a group of understory plants, then the fallen leaves serve as a natural mulch.

How much lawn should be removed from around a lawn tree? It depends upon your situation and the size of your yard, but a good rule of thumb is to use the leaf drop area as a guideline for the minimum no-lawn space. That way, the future leaves will drop into the new lawn-free area, which will promote healthier soil that will better support the tree.

Removing lawn from around trees has to be done by hand because you can't kill the grass using herbicide, thick mulch, solarization, or sod cutter without damaging the tree. I usually use a claw or cultivator to catch and pull out the long runners of the St. Augustine grass, but the bunching grasses may require a different removal tool. Either way, take note of where the tree's main surface roots are located. Depending upon your plans for plants, it might make sense to dig out holes in the spaces between the roots when you find them to help you visualize where to plant the understory vegetation.

What to plant around the tree? This depends on the tree species, whether it's evergreen or deciduous, the density of its shade, and its form. If low branches are in place, you might plant just native ferns near the tree, because it will probably be too shady for anything else. Farther out from the tree, it's a good idea to plant a variety of native understory plants including shrubs, small understory trees, bunching grasses, and ground covers. This is how to build a habitat grove, which I'll describe as I discuss trees, but for our discussion on lawns, make the edge of this grove easy to mow, with wide-sweeping curves and with no vertical sides.

Other areas suitable for lawn removal include areas next to fences, tool sheds or other outbuildings, and in sunny areas where you could grow vegetables. You don't need to do it all at once. Do what we did: work on removing lawn little by little as you have the time and energy.

Replacing Lawn with Ground Covers

There are quite a few options for nonlawn landscapes, but for areas where you want a lawnlike landscape for openness and visibility to a view or for safety, here are two tough native ground covers to consider:

Sunshine mimosa or powderpuff (*Mimosa strigillosa*) is a vining ground cover that makes a great lawn alternative in locations that are mostly sunny, and it takes moderate foot traffic. It has pretty pink flower heads that are borne on five-inch stalks. Because it is a legume and fixes nitrogen, it will grow in nutrient-poor soil. While it does take a while to become established, it stays low enough so it can be mowed several times per year to keep the other plants cut back while it's filling in. After it's established, an annual mowing is probably all that will be needed.

Fogfruit (*Phyla nodiflora*) is also a vining ground cover that makes a great lawn alternative and takes moderate foot traffic. Once established, it is drought tolerant, salt tolerant, and tolerant of a wide range of conditions, from dry to wet. It's also called capeweed, turkeytangle, or matchweed. The last name is for the flower heads, which have a purple center surrounded by tiny white flowers; the heads are the size and shape of a match head. Some people trim it back with a string trimmer once or twice a year for a neater and denser texture. In addition to supporting pollinators, it also serves as a larval host plant for some butterflies.

I know one gardener who was excited to start some fogfruit in her yard. She bought several containers of this plant at a native plant sale run by her local native plant chapter. When she got home and was figuring out the best place to start this native ground cover, she was surprised to find that it was already growing in her yard.

For both of these ground covers and for other crawling plants, when runners trail out onto sidewalks or driveways, don't cut them off; instead, bend them back onto themselves. This reduces maintenance chores, because each cut runner will produce two new runners in that spot, while a runner bent back into the ground cover will be growing away from the edge and create a more solid cover.

Sunshine mimosa (*Mimosa strigillosa*) provides a beautiful and tough ground cover and is often used as a lawn substitute in sunny and mostly sunny areas of the landscape. It can tolerate moderate foot traffic.

Fogfruit (*Phyla nodiflora*) is common throughout the state and will quickly cover bare soil with its runners.

Lawn Irrigation Strategies

One of our first purchases when we moved to Florida was a good rain gauge. Rain is variable here, and you can't rely on the local weather services or apps to report the actual rainfall on your yard. Dean keeps track of the rainfall. The idea is to know how much total water is delivered to your landscape by the local weather and by irrigation. Here's how we tested our automated irrigation system: We measured the total water that fell when running the system for fifteen minutes using various straight-sided containers placed in several spots. The amount of water collected in them let us know how long to run each section of the system to deliver the desired amount.

During the growing season, most established lawns do fine with about ¾ inch of rain per week. During the five-month wet season, supplemental irrigation is rarely needed. Then, in the winter months from November through March, we let the lawn go into dormancy and do not irrigate or mow. We run the irrigation system only when needed, and now our lawn has a much lighter footprint on the planet than when we moved in.

So do your homework and be smart about using just enough irrigation to keep your landscape from drying up during droughts. If you have an automated irrigation system, don't just set it and forget it, because then it will waste lots of our precious water.

The Grass Really Can Be Greener

This new paradigm of smaller, nonpoisoned lawns saves time and money, and they're safe for you, your kids, and your pets 100 percent of the time. In addition, nonpoisoned and diverse lawns support various butterflies and native bees. We need less lawn in our neighborhoods to help wildlife and to preserve our precious water supply. As gardeners, we need to get on those HOA boards of governors to help modify the regulations to ease up on lawn restrictions, to promote water conservation, and to improve the environment (it's a no-grass roots movement, maybe). In my opinion, we should leave the fine turf for all those golf courses, but even at golf courses, there has been a movement to reduce turf in unplayable areas and to increase sustainability overall.

Florida's Water Management Districts

Florida's five water management districts have regulations and public outreach campaigns recommending less lawn irrigation. At this time, our district, the St. Johns River Water Management District, limits general outdoor irrigation to once a week during the winter (defined as when we are on Eastern Standard Time) and twice a week during Eastern Daylight Time. These restrictions are in effect for all irrigation systems, whether the water comes from shallow wells, lakes (like ours), or the municipal water supply. In order to monitor compliance, we are limited to watering only certain days of the week, depending upon whether our house numbers are odd or even. There are also regulations for automated systems. For example, they must include a moisture detector, so the system doesn't go through its cycles if there has been a recent rain; also, the water source must be the lowest-quality water available. (We live on a dammed, spring-fed lake, and all the irrigation systems in the neighborhood use lake water for irrigation.)

The water districts are part of Florida's Department of Environmental Protection, which has many other responsibilities. You can find out more on the department's website, https://floridadep.gov.

Many Florida homeowners have automated, built-in irrigation systems. Unfortunately, many of these systems are in the "set & forget" mode and millions of gallons of our precious water supply is wasted.

4

~

Pollinator Gardens

Creating attractive spaces for butterflies, moths, native bees, and other bugs is a rewarding way to replace some of your lawn. One thing that's different about Florida pollinator gardens is that to best support the pollinators, we need something blooming all year long, because even in North Florida, warm days will occur in winter. Some butterflies may emerge during those warm days and will need sources of pollen and nectar to sustain them.

Many native bees and wasps are more active pollinators than the butterflies and the moths. In addition, many of the wasps are effective predators of pest insects, so having a good pollinator garden will keep these beneficial insects nearby. While wasps and bees may have had a bad reputation, the vast majority have solitary nests and are not aggressive. Their nests are generally unseen and unnoticed in our yards, because these creatures are too darn busy to pay us any mind.

In other words, to build a pollinator-friendly habitat, you provide nectar sources with a variety of flowers all year long for the adult butterflies and other pollinators, food for the larvae (caterpillars), shallow puddles or mudflats for the male butterflies and the mud-dauber wasps, and areas of thick vegetation for shelter. The insects that we invite to our plants during the warm months also need places to overwinter. Some drill tiny holes into dead stems where they overwinter as adults, larvae, or in their egg stage, while other insect species overwinter in leaf litter, bark, or under the ground. So go easy on the fall maintenance for the best pollinator habitat.

When you work to attract pollinators, you'll be supporting populations of other beneficial critters such as bats, lizards, frogs, toads, and birds. Some birds survive on insects alone and catch insects in midair or forage for them on tree bark, leaves, twigs, and stems, and in leaf litter. Even birds that do not typically eat insects as adults feed insects, particularly caterpillars, to their young: insects provide easy-to-digest, optimal nutrition for growth. In turn, the birds help to control garden pests. It's all about balance, so when you supply insect-friendly habitat, it forms the basis for the rest of the ecosystem on up through the food chain to top predators such as hawks.

No Landscape-Wide Poisons

The first thing to do to create good pollinator habitat is to stop using all landscape-wide pesticides. I discussed the typical lawn-care mixture of pesticides earlier, but it's worth reiterating that for our pollinator gardens, the worst parts of that mixture are the insecticides. They are active for several days after the application and will kill your pollinators, especially the native bees and wasps that mostly nest in the ground. They will also kill the predator bugs and the benign bugs that all have roles to play in the local ecosystem.

The other pesticides that may not be as obvious are the broadleaf weed killers, such as the systemic herbicide 2,4-D (2,4-Dichlorophenoxyacetic acid), which are sprayed on lawns to selectively kill the nongrass plants. These herbicides could drift onto your pollinator plants. I know of a native society chapter that had installed and maintained a pollinator garden at a local hospital for years. One day, they went to do some weeding and to install some new plants, but all the plants in the pollinator garden had shriveled up—they looked the same as the weeds dying in the lawn. So the lawn-care people had probably sprayed the herbicide on a windy day and killed the pollinator plants. The garden had to be replanted. It was pretty discouraging, but the hospital acknowledged the problem and paid for the new plants since the garden had been so popular for their patients and staff. Hopefully, they also stopped the lawn pesticides.

What about the Pest Bugs?

Without those landscape-wide insecticides, many of the plants we use to attract pollinators might also attract aphids, other sucking bugs, and other herbivores. Often the "expert" advice is that if you wish to avoid toxic poisons, spray homemade concoctions with soap or detergent to get rid of the aphids. Don't do this, either!

All terrestrial plants have waxy, hydrophobic cuticles. You've probably noticed water beading into droplets on plant surfaces after a rain or first thing on a cool morning. This is the cuticle at work. Some plants with thicker cuticles repel water more readily, but all terrestrial plants produce this protective layer. The cuticle is the plant's defense against desiccation, pathogen infestation, and UV radiation; it also deters some herbivore activity.

The casual and oft-repeated suggestion to use insecticidal soap and other soapy mixtures is shortsighted, because the plant's cuticle will be dissolved, at least to some extent. The plant, which may already have been stressed by the aphids, may not have the spare energy to form a new cuticle. With a damaged cuticle, the plant will wilt more often, and without its normal turgidity, even more types of pests will be able to attack it. With a damaged cuticle, the plant may be sunburned, and the burned tissue is an opening for fungi and bacteria to enter. In the end, the soap-treated plant is much more vulnerable to damage than before this treatment.

Soaps and detergents disturb the balance in working ecosystems because they serve as poisons in your landscape's ecosystem. Yes, they may wipe out the aphids for a while, but in addition to leaving your plants vulnerable to additional damage, they will also wipe out or chase away their predators. The ladybugs (both the larval and adult stages), assassin bugs, praying mantises, and predatory wasps will not have their food. And the predators for those bugs, such as dragonflies, lizards, bats, and insect-eating birds, will not have their food, either. Your yard's ecosystem is a tangled web, and your intervention against one member will have an impact on that whole web of relationships.

Butterfly and Moth Life Cycles

The egg. An adult female lays her eggs on the right plants for the caterpillars to eat when they hatch from the eggs. Some butterflies and moths lay their eggs on only one type of plant! To determine if it's the right plant, they taste the leaves with their feet before laying the eggs.

The caterpillar. When the egg hatches, a tiny caterpillar emerges and eats its own egg casing first. It then starts to eat the plant, but if the plant has been treated with systemic insecticide, it will die as soon as it begins to eat. The caterpillar stage is when most of the eating and growing occurs in the insect's life cycle. Each time the caterpillar gets too big for its skin, it sheds or molts to begin a new stage. These different stages between molts are called instars. Most moths and butterflies go through about five instars before they reach their final stage. Between the stages, the larva will have grown bigger, but it may also be different colors or have possibly grown hairs, spines, bristles, or maybe a hornlike structure at one end of its body. The juvenile stages are when they are most at risk, because birds feed these easy-to-digest morsels to their young. Some caterpillars disguise themselves by camouflage coloration or by staying on the underside of the leaves so they are hard to see, while others have a warning coloration that lets birds know they taste bad or may be toxic if eaten.

The metamorphosis. The last time the caterpillar sheds, a hard casing forms around it that is called a chrysalis or pupa. Moths may also spin a silky cocoon. Chemicals are released from the insect's body that change and rearrange all the cells to create the adult form with wings. For butterflies and moths in warm climates, the transformation can be completed in ten to fifteen days, depending on the size. But where there are cold winters, the insect may overwinter in this stage and emerge when the weather warms in spring. This is called diapause, and some of them can wait for several years inside their chrysalis until the conditions are right to emerge! But this doesn't happen in Florida, with our warm cycles in winter, the butterflies and moths could emerge at any time, so this is why we need year-round flowers.

The adult. When the butterfly or moth emerges, it needs to plump up its wings first, filling them with fluid and then letting them dry and harden. The adults can reproduce, fly in search of food, and even migrate if necessary. In the case of some moths, such as the luna moth (*Actias luna*), the adult does not have functional mouthparts and cannot eat. In its short but beautiful adult stage, its only agenda is to reproduce.

If You Must Intervene . . .

If the infestation is really intense, use only water to rinse away the aphids and other bugs. This way the plant retains its cuticle, and you can reduce the aphids on the plants without killing the aphids or their predators. Your goal, as a pollinator gardener, is to help your yard become a working ecosystem.

Insects go through various life stages, and as ecosystem gardeners, it helps to learn to recognize the various life stages. Most people are aware of butterflies and moths, with their caterpillars and pupae, but others you may be aware of are the mosquitoes and dragonflies, whose larvae are naiads that must live in water to complete their life cycles. But many other bugs are probably less well-known. For example, you should know that the larval stages of ladybugs (lady beetles) look nothing like the adults. They look sinister, not like beneficial aphid-killing friends. But ladybugs, throughout their larval and adult stages, are voracious predators, and each individual will devour approximately five thousand aphids. It's an adjustment to change our attitude to overcome years of hearing that all bugs are bad and must be poisoned. But learning about the bugs that are good for our gardens helps us to turn our yards into working ecosystems.

Support All Life Stages of Pollinators

To support the adult pollinators, choose an assortment of native plants with a variety of flower and flower head structures. You'll need broad flower heads, like those in the aster family, to support large-bodied pollinators, smaller flowers or flower heads for tiny insects, and tubular flowers for pollinators with long proboscis parts and for hummingbirds. You'll need flowers that are open during the day and some that are open at night. And as previously mentioned, it's best to have something blooming all year long.

It's best to group bunches of the same plant species together within your pollinator garden to create masses of single colors, rather than many colors mixed together like a checkerboard. Insects see color differently than we do, in part because they can perceive ultraviolet light. It's been shown that butterflies prefer large swaths of color.

Most adult insects are able to extract the nectar or pollen they need from a variety of plants, but the same is not true for larval food sources. Many butterflies and moths have adapted to feed on certain plants as caterpillars. Often these insects can tolerate plants with certain toxins, storing the chemicals in their tissues, which gives both the larvae and the adults the advantage of being toxic or tasting bad, so birds learn not to eat them. Probably the best-known example is the monarch butterfly (*Danaus plexippus*), which lays its eggs only on milkweed plants (*Asclepias* spp.), whose bitter substances are transferred to the caterpillars. There are twenty-one milkweed species native to Florida, so we have many ways to support these beautiful butterflies.

There are many other relationships that you'll want to know, like the six native passionflower species (*Passiflora* spp.), which are the host plants for both the zebra longwing (*Heliconius charithonia*), our state butterfly, and the gulf fritillary (*Agraulis vanillae*). If you are looking to attract a particular butterfly or moth, you can determine the larval food sources on the Butterflies and Moths of North America website, www.butterfliesandmoths.org.

Real butterfly gardeners cheer when something eats their plants.

LOCATION, LOCATION, LOCATION!

Insects are cold-blooded animals and usually become active only after the sun has warmed the air, so locate the majority of your pollinator gardens in the full sun. Fortunately, the pollinator plants also prefer full sun; this is probably not an accident, but part of the ancient evolutionary connections between plants and animals. If possible, build several pollinator habitats around your yard instead of just one big one. One goal is to have some flowers in the morning sun and others that catch the later afternoon sun, so the pollinators can find good sources of food through more of the day.

Enjoying the Pollinators

One consideration in locating pollinator gardens is to place them where you and your family can enjoy the show, because while flowers

Passionflower (*Passiflora incarnata*) supports both zebra longwing butterfly larvae (white with black hairs) and the gulf fritillary butterfly larvae (reddish-brown with black hairs). If it's in partial shade, you're more likely to host zebra longwings, but if it's in full sun, you're more likely to host gulf fritillaries.

are pretty, it's the pollinators that bring life to the landscape. Pollinator gardens are much more interesting than boring gardens filled with plants from other parts of the world that do not play much of a role in the local ecosystem. As Doug Tallamy's research shows, many of those alien plants might as well be plastic when it comes to the life cycles of the native pollinators.

Here's an example of how pollinators compelled us to change our landscape. When we first moved into the house, the previous owners had filled the bed along the back, southwest-facing wall of the house and a sidewalk with roses and Mexican heather shrubs. I decided that just outside the back door from the kitchen would be the perfect place for an herb garden. I planted a rosemary bush, Greek oregano, sage, mint, chives, dill, and basil. The herbs did well there because of the hot afternoon sun. This bed also happens to be our view out the kitchen window where we eat most of our meals. A couple of years later, after I'd introduced various natives into our landscape, some tropical sage

(*Salvia coccinea*) had planted itself into the herb garden. Well, those scarlet blooms attracted an ongoing parade of pollinators, including butterflies, bees, wasps, and hummingbirds. They were much more fun to watch than the herb garden. I moved the herbs to a bed near the garage and planted more pollinator-friendly wildflowers outside our window. It didn't happen all at once. The rosemary stayed for a few more years. We have loved watching the ongoing pollinator party in our wildflower garden right outside our kitchen window.

Pollinators for Vegetable Gardens

For many of our crops where we consume a fruit or seed, pollination is required. Prime examples of this are the members of the squash family—squashes, cucumbers, melons, and pumpkins—because there are separate male and female flowers on each plant, and the female flower needs to be pollinated seven to ten times before a fruit will develop. If a female flower is not pollinated, the small start of a fruit at the base of the flower will not expand, turn yellow, and then fall off the vine. I discuss this later, in the chapter on growing foods, but any discussion of pollinators must mention that if you want to grow crops, you'll need pollinator plants nearby, so there will be a ready pollinator population as soon as your crops begin to bloom. It's a good idea to plant some flowers such as marigolds and nasturtiums as crops and among your other crops since their flowers are edible and attract the pollinators. You could also add some large containers of pollinator plants that can be placed close to your crops. Also, it's good to have some more permanent pollinator gardens not too far away.

From Stump to Butterfly Garden

Here's a saga of one pollinator garden. The 2004 hurricanes took out several trees in our yard. One was a sweetgum tree (*Liquidambar styraciflua*) in the middle of our backyard, which left a stump there. We transformed this eyesore to a beautiful butterfly garden. First, we cut away all the turf around the stump until we had a circle that was about six feet in diameter, then we dumped several wheelbarrow loads of pond muck on top of the stump. (We were cleaning out the front pond at the time, but you could use any compost—even a large pile of dead leaves covered with some soil.) Then we covered the muck with a few inches of sandy soil. The resulting mound was about two and a half feet taller than the lawn. The old stump would eventually rot and provide nutrients for our butterfly island.

That first year I planted some mystery tubers that the former owner had planted in with the canna lilies (*Canna × generalis*) on the side of the house. Later, I figured out that these were hidden ginger lilies (*Curcuma petiolata*). The tropical-looking ginger lily leaves were three feet tall, so I planted several of them and several canna lilies in the center or the top of the mound, where they provided a good backdrop for everything else that was planted there. Those big leaves die back in the winter.

Over the years, I tried several types of plants on the mound with varying degrees of success, and we removed a little more of the lawn several times, so the mound was expanded along the way. I've also added compost and mulched the mound to keep some of the weeds at bay. The first few years, I planted zinnias (*Zinnia elegans*), which grew very well there and attracted a good variety of pollinators. Some soft rushes (*Juncus effusus*) volunteered on the far side (and wetter side) of the mound, and while the rushes don't add much to the butterfly habitat, they provide a year-round vertical structure. I planted some perennial Maximilian sunflowers (*Helianthus maximiliani*) on the top of the mound, and they reseeded themselves for a couple of years. Some rice button asters (*Symphyotrichum dumosum*) volunteered as they have in various parts of our yard—they don't look like much until late fall. The pollinators love those tiny flower heads when many others have died back.

To reduce ongoing maintenance, I began to shift from annuals like zinnias to a mixture of native perennials; they make it easier to provide a dependable variety of nectar for the butterflies and hummingbirds. My goal was to get to the point where all that was required is a quick mulching each year for our butterfly and hummingbird paradise. It was an interesting exercise that shifted dramatically ten years later, when I ripped it all out, doubled the size of the mound, and transplanted my three highbush blueberries to the mound. While there is now a

The 2004 hurricanes took out a sweetgum tree (*Liquidambar styraciflua*) in the middle of our back yard. Its stump became the base of a butterfly mound. In the background you can see the vegetable bed on the southwest side of the house, where we were growing tomatoes and peppers at that time.

A couple of years later we had a beautiful butterfly garden growing on top of the stump. The meadow area behind the mound is the one discussed in the section on lawns, where we just stopped mowing to make a meadow. This is what it looked like a few years later.

fringe of pollinator plants around the feet of the blueberry shrubs, the mound is now called Blueberry Hill. (More on Florida blueberries in the chapter on growing food.) The various transformations of this area in our backyard provide just one example of how managing a landscape is an ongoing adventure, not a one-time event.

Pollinator-Friendly Meadows

Most natural meadows tend to be dominated by grasses, rushes, and sedges in differing proportions depending upon the native ecosystem in that area and the drainage. If it's wetter on a seasonal basis, there will be more rushes and sedges. There will be other volunteers as well. Here in northeastern Florida, my volunteers include rice button aster (*Symphyotrichum dumosum*), goldenrods (*Solidago* spp.), lyre-leaf sage (*Salvia lyrata*), forked bluecurls (*Trichostema dichotomum*), Spanish needles (*Bidens alba*), and dogfennel (*Eupatorium capillifolium*), all of which the pollinators love.

In some meadow areas, I've supplemented the volunteers by sowing various wildflower seeds and installing clusters of native plants. The best time to plant the wildflower seedlings is when you have time to water them and weed around them until they are well established, but most people do this in early spring. The best time to sow most wildflower seeds is in late fall or early winter. I tried a can of wildflower seed mix early on, but most of those flowers were non-natives like oriental poppy (*Papaver orientale*), forget-me-nots (*Myosotis* spp.), and sweet alyssum (*Lobularia maritima*). Now, I use real Florida wildflower seeds from the Florida Wildflowers Growers Cooperative; see www.floridawildflowers.com.

I have planted seed in meadows without doing any preparation, which would be like a natural reseeding, but I've found that a bit of preparation, including some selective weeding, scratching the surface of the soil between the meadow plants where I want the wildflowers, and then hand irrigating them after planting produces a better outcome. I'vc also sowed the seeds in beds where everything has been cleaned out, covering them with a thin pine needle mulch, and then transplanting the seedlings out to the meadow in the spring. You could

Rice button asters (*Symphyotrichum dumosum*) make for quite a show and attract many pollinators in the late fall with their masses of lavender flower heads.

also sow the seeds in flats so you can keep a closer eye on them through the winter, including some supplemental irrigation through the dry season, before transplanting them into meadows or pollinator gardens.

Any method you use to increase the native wildflower populations into the meadow will help create a more pollinator-friendly and more attractive meadow. Over the years some of those wildflowers will die out, but others will last longer and some will self-seed. Of course, you could reseed those wildflowers that need renewal, or you could let nature take its course.

Ongoing meadow maintenance can include an annual trimming at about six or eight inches in early spring. Don't do this in the fall, because as previously discussed, many insects need those flower and grass stalks to hide out for the winter. And as we did for our front meadow, you may need to dig out the tree saplings that volunteer, so it doesn't transform into forest. Much of Florida consists of fire-controlled ecosystems; while we can't usually burn our meadows in an urban or suburban neighborhood, the annual trimming serves a similar purpose.

Our Yard Is a Pollinator-Friendly Habitat

Over the years, we've built areas of habitat in a variety of places around the yard. All those pollinators we've supported have provided food for birds, and the small birds became food for the hawks. The workings of our yard's ecosystem provides us with endless entertainment so that each walk into our yard has the potential to become a delightful adventure in nature.

5

❧

Florida's Trees and Shrubs

Trees are especially important in Florida because they provide shade, and through their transpiration process, they actually cool the air. At 68°F, each gram of water that evaporates removes 585 calories (a measure of heat) from the ambient air temperature. In addition, trees provide habitat for birds and other wildlife, and they enhance the typical homeowner's real estate value. But Florida's trees offer us transplanted gardeners even more with their wide diversity, unique habits, and habitats. Even so, there will be some trees that will be familiar such as the red maple (*Acer rubrum*), which is native to all of eastern North America, including all but the southernmost counties of Florida. Even though they are all the same species, make sure you purchase only those that are bred from Florida stock, because a red maple from Vermont would be totally out of synch in Florida. Florida's maples bloom in early February and their leaves emerge soon after, while a maple from Vermont would be months behind.

The "Bones" of Your Landscape

Trees and shrubs, the woody plants, provide the most obvious structure, or the "bones," of the landscape. In Florida we have hundreds of wonderful trees and shrubs from which to choose. The most sustainable action is to preserve the appropriate existing woody plants on your property, and then, when selecting new trees and shrubs, to do as your extension agent would advise: "Select the right plant for the right place." With proper selection and maintenance, your woody plants will provide shade, privacy, and habitat for wildlife. They prevent erosion, cool their surroundings, and absorb carbon dioxide from the air. That trees and shrubs also add beauty and value to any landscape is a lovely bonus.

EVALUATING EXISTING TREES AND SHRUBS

Evaluating existing woody plants in your landscape is an important initial step in prudent and sustainable landscape design. Preserving your existing trees, if they are in good health and growing in appropriate locations, is smart. However, large trees that have been weakened by disease, old age, injured roots, or physical restrictions, such as sidewalks, foundations, or roads may need to be pruned or removed before they do harm. Periodic evaluations of this kind help prepare your landscape for hurricanes and other strong storms. Note: Many trees in Florida live in harmony with other plants such as Spanish moss (*Tillandsia usneoides*), resurrection fern (*Pleopeltis polypodioides*), mistletoe (*Phoradendron leucarpum*), and more. These plants do not need to be removed. For details, see below for "What's Growing on Your Oak?"

If you have a lot of trees and don't know where to start, seek professional advice from a certified arborist who can help you develop a sound management plan. An arborist may recommend pruning to relieve stress on the trunk. The process may take several years because no more than 20 percent of a tree should be trimmed out in one year, and topping is never a good option. Some of your more dangerous and inappropriately placed trees may need to be removed, but work to preserve as many woody plants in your landscape as you can, because a small replacement tree may take twenty years or more to begin to provide as many benefits as your mature trees. Be sure to also have the arborist identify all your trees and shrubs for you. Be advised that someone who cuts down trees is not necessarily a certified arborist. Find a certified arborist near you at www.isa-arbor.com.

ARRANGING WOODY PLANTS

Before you dig any holes, call 811 or go to www.sunshine811.com to locate underground utility lines and keep trees away from this infrastructure. Develop a plan for your trees. Ideally, you'd create a scale drawing of your lot and plan out different sections to suit your purposes for each area, but a quick sketch may work well for a simple landscape without too much slope. Also, because some trees are adapted for growing in periodic standing water and some are not, analyze stormwater drainage and other water flows. If you decide to build rain gardens and French drains to handle most of the stormwater most of the time, do so before you plant your new trees and shrubs. (More on this in the chapter "Stormwater Management.")

Grouping compatible trees and shrubs together into groves provides an arrangement that is more wind resistant than single or stand-alone trees. Your plan should consider prevailing winds and wind sheltering, especially for coastal locations, since the constant onshore winds carry so much salt. This is important here in Florida, because no matter where you are in the Sunshine State, hurricanes will come blasting through eventually. While the coastal areas are more vulnerable, nowhere is immune. Our house is about thirty miles from the Atlantic Coast and sixty miles from the Gulf Coast and we've still suffered damage. Our first year here in Florida, four hurricanes rumbled through, and we were without power for ten days, twice. We lost several trees that year; most of them were single trees that had been left from the forested area when they built our house and were surrounded by lawn. And while there are no guarantees when it comes to hurricanes, some planning on wind resistance, also called hurricane-scaping, can make a big difference.

Also, groves of compatible trees and shrubs are more drought tolerant than single specimens, and this arrangement provides good habitat for each other and for wildlife. The goal is to imitate how those plants would have been positioned naturally, and then mulch the whole area to create a grove. The first few years will probably require some prudent weeding to keep out the invasive plants and aggressive volunteers. This provides room for the desirable plants that you've planted and those that have volunteered. Once the plants start working together and the soil is disturbed less often, less and less maintenance will be needed.

Choosing Trees and Shrubs

When choosing the ideal trees and shrubs for your landscape, plants native to your specific region are the best place to start. Native plants have a well-developed tolerance for Florida's soil, pests, salt air, and its wet and dry seasons. When considering which trees and shrubs will fit into your landscape plans, think years ahead about how much space the mature trees and shrubs will require, vertically and horizontally, then add 30 percent to the estimated horizontal growth (dripline) to estimate the root mass.

When purchasing new trees and shrubs, it's best if you can select your specimens from a reputable local nursery that can offer good advice along with its well-cared-for plants. When choosing trees, look for those with one main trunk or those that could be pruned to a main trunk over a few years. For most species, a one-trunked tree will look better in the long run, be more wind resistant, and require less corrective pruning. Look at the roots: they should be firm and white, and they should not be circling within the pot or rooted into the soil beneath the pot. In general, you'll want a young, untopped tree with healthy roots. Look for new growth or buds and good green color on the older leaves.

The old advice was to choose the largest trees you could afford, but smaller trees, both native and non-native, require less long-term care, especially when it comes to irrigation. They are more likely to survive and may even outgrow larger, more expensive trees within just a couple of years.

Planting Procedures

When planting a tree, dig a hole that is two or three inches shallower than its root ball or pot and at least twice as wide: wider is better. Be sure that the center of the hole provides a solid footing, so the tree won't sink once it's in place. Most trees have a slight flare where the roots start to spread; size your hole so that this flare will be slightly

This winged elm (*Ulmus alata*) had been held in a one-gallon container for way too long. I rinsed away all away the growing medium, which revealed its circling roots. I corrected these by stretching them out and staking them in the planting hole in the spreading position. I cracked one of the larger roots in the process. I added the rich growing medium that had been in the pot to the compost pile—not to the planting hole. Both of these actions encourage tree roots to grow outward. Ten years after planting this tree, and after carefully pruning it over several years to a single leader, it is more than twenty-five feet tall.

above the soil line. Just so you know, trees grown from cuttings will not have such a flare.

Before you remove the tree from its pot or wrap, set it in the hole to check for placement. Prop it up if necessary, and then stand back to view it from all angles; look up as well—you don't want to plant trees directly under or near power lines. Also, go inside and view it from your windows to make sure your planned location does not block a prized view. Again, remember to consider its mature size.

Only after all this checking, remove it from its pot and rinse away the old soil from the root ball. As you place the tree into the hole, stretch out its roots. Fill the hole with water as you gently shovel the native soil back into the hole. Gently tamp the soil in place to make sure that there are no air pockets. No amendments to the soil are recommended for trees or palms. It's been shown that fertilizers, compost and other soil-enhancing materials added to the planting hole can discourage the roots from spreading out into surrounding soil. The root rinsing should be done for container-grown trees or shrubs—not field-grown trees or transplanted trees. For more information on the science behind root rinsing, see Linda Chalker-Scott's "Horticultural Myths" page at www.informedgardener.com.

After the hole has been filled in, press the soil gently in place and create a shallow saucer equal to or larger than the diameter of the root ball by creating a berm of soil two or three inches high around the circumference—this ensures that the irrigation water soaks into the planting hole. Lay two to three inches of mulch over this whole saucer area, but never up against the trunk.

If the tree is wobbly and could be knocked over by a gust of wind, staking may be necessary until the roots start growing. Make sure that no stakes enter the root ball and that no wires or ropes abrade the trunk. Except for palms, stake the tree in such a way that the trunk can bend slightly in the wind: this will enable the tree to build strength in its trunk. Remove the stakes as soon as the tree has stabilized so that it stands on its own. This way the tree can build its own strength. Newly transplanted palms, however, should always be held in place firmly for several months because they must grow a whole new root system.

Do not prune the tree for at least a year after planting, because it will need all the energy it can get to grow new roots to adjust to its new space, and it gets that energy from its leaves. When you do begin to prune it, to encourage a single stem and good shape, cut no more than 20 percent each year. If you're in an area where deer roam, it's a good idea to protect young trees with wire fence cages to protect them. If the trees are in a meadow area, the wire cage also prevents accidental mowing or trimming.

Irrigation for Newly Planted Trees

Your transplanted trees need a soaking rain of one inch or more per week for several months. If there are no consistent, soaking rains, here's what to do. General landscape irrigation is not enough. You could set up a temporary drip irrigation system to water your newly planted trees, especially if you've installed a lot of them, or you could irrigate manually.

Each time you irrigate, it's best to water with three gallons per inch of trunk caliper (the diameter of the trunk at six inches above the root ball of saplings). For example, use six gallons for a two-inch caliper tree. Apply slowly, so all the water soaks into the planting hole.

If a tree is one- to two-caliper inches, the best practice is to water daily for a few weeks and every other day for the next two months. After that, water weekly until the tree is established and shows new growth. For trees more than three-caliper inches and for palms, the best practice is to water daily for six weeks; every other day for the next five months; and weekly after that until the tree is established and new growth doesn't wilt during dry periods.

After the initial period, continue to supplement irrigation for your tree during drought conditions for at least a year—two or more years is better for larger specimens. If you can't arrange for this much irrigation, choose smaller trees for better success. They usually catch up to the larger specimens within a couple of years and save a lot of time, water, and money.

When your tree has been in the ground for at least three months, or just before its next growth period, you could apply a topdressing of compost or a light application of a slow-release, organic fertilizer, such as fish emulsion, around the outside of the planting hole to improve the soil there. Don't dig it in—this is a top dressing. If you do this again, the next ring of compost should be a little further away each time. The idea of improving the soil outside the planting hole is to entice the roots to grow outward, and this makes the trees both more wind tolerant and more drought tolerant. This is important here in Florida.

My Magnificent but Messy Magnolias

Our first Florida tree adventure was dealing with the two southern magnolias (*Magnolia grandiflora*) that the previous owner had planted in the middle of our front lawn. While magnolias seem to typify southern elegance for most people, very little grows under that spreading and shallow-rooted tree, and the ground is littered with piles of leathery leaves and the woody conelike flower cores that drop all year long. That elegant tree is a messy one. My landscape professor used to say that the southern magnolia is a fabulous tree, but not in the middle of your yard, because neither lawn nor bedding flowers will grow under it. Plant it in a location where its litter will not destroy lawns or gardens.

The house was only two years old when we moved in, and it looked like the previous owners might have purchased these trees at a local store where I noticed trees close to this size. One was about fifteen feet tall and the other about twelve. I assumed that since they'd been planted so recently, they would not have grown too far beyond the original root balls. So shortly after we moved in, with my professor's advice ringing in my ears, I decided that the two magnolias needed to be moved.

I pruned the roots and some of the low branches of each tree in June, so they'd have a chance to recover and grow new roots close to the trunk before I transplanted them that fall. To prune the roots, I cut down to the depth of the blade of a regular garden shovel all around at the edge of the mulched area. Then I repeated the trip around the circle with a long-bladed spade. In the end, I'd made an eighteen-inch-deep slice around both trees.

When fall came with its cooler weather, it was time to move the magnolias. I decided to plant them out by the front fence at the edge of the oaks, where they'd get good light and have enough space to do what they wanted. My thought was that we could still enjoy the magnolias, but not have to deal with their litter in the lawn.

The first step was to dig holes in the new locations just as deep as the estimated root mass. Then I scraped off the mulch from around the trunk, recut the roots at the edge of the mulch line, and dug out soil from under the dense mass of surface roots. In order not to make a mess on the grass, and to retain as much soil as possible for refilling the hole, I placed the soil on a tarp. We used another tarp to transport the trees to their new locations.

Because the trees were so big, Dean and I both worked to move them. We tipped each tree and its roots up and out of the hole. We both dug some more to retain as many of the roots as possible. None of the roots seemed to be any thicker than a half-inch or so. With a lot of effort, especially for the fifteen-foot tree, we rolled each one on its side and onto the tarp. Then, like a couple of field mules pulling a plow, we dragged them to their new planting holes. The holes needed reshaping

The southern magnolias (*M. grandiflora*) shed their leaves all year long, so they create a messy leaf drop on the lawn. We decided to move them.

once we tried to fit the root masses into them, because the root masses were larger than estimated.

We flooded the holes as we filled in with local soil only, making sure that there were no big air pockets. After we checked to see that each tree was vertical, we tamped down the soil along the edges of the surface root mass and built a berm of soil around the plant hole to hold any water. I hand irrigated each of them with a full three-gallon watering can daily for a few weeks and tapered off to three times per week for another couple of months while waiting for significant rainfall. I was not used to such a dry fall. This extra irrigation is important because most of the trees' root hairs were torn off during transplant, meaning that they would have a more difficult time absorbing water.

The trees survived the move, and fifteen years later, they are more than thirty feet tall and are a lovely addition to our front meadow and woods with their gloriously large, white, grandiflora blooms. And we never had to rake up those darn leathery leaves again. But in hindsight, I probably should have let them stay in place. I should have removed the lawn from around them and planted native azaleas and other acid-loving native trees and shrubs around and in between those trees to create a natural grove, where their leaves would have merely acted as a natural mulch. That way, the magnolias would have been closer, and we could better appreciate their wonderful blooms.

Another reason I wish we'd kept the magnolias where they were is that the neighbors across the street later removed the piney forest in front of their house to build a garage/office and a raised septic drain field. They did install some native cabbage palms and magnolias, but having those magnolias with understory shrubs there would have provided better screening. Oh, for a crystal ball!

In addition to the two southern magnolias in front, there were some naturally occurring southern magnolias and sweetbay magnolias (*M. virginiana*) growing at the edges of wooded areas in the front, side, and back yards. The latter species, a lovely smaller magnolia, often gets lost in the shuffle when compared to its more glorious relative. Its silver-backed leaves and highly fragrant, night-blooming flowers are about half the size of southern magnolia's, but this tree is a lot neater. It keeps its leaves through the winter here in Florida and loses them all at once in the spring as the new leaves are emerging. The sweetbay, also called the swamp magnolia, is often found growing in standing water. It does have a tendency to produce thicket-forming suckers around itself, so keep that in mind if you plant it. Both of these magnolias are native to Florida, but the range of the sweetbay extends north into Pennsylvania while southern magnolia's native range extends only to the northern border of North Carolina. Both, however, are often planted much farther north. Many had been planted around Annapolis, Maryland, and during the thirty years I lived in that region, I'd always wanted them, but my yard there was too small. Now, I have many magnolias and have transplanted quite a number of them over the years when they sprouted in inconvenient places. Mostly, I've added them to the side yard to provide a denser screen between our yard and our neighbor's.

FLORIDA'S PALMS

What would the Florida landscape be without palm trees? Our state tree is the cabbage palm (*Sabal palmetto*); a number of other palms and palmettos are native to Florida, too. Those gracefully curved trunks and topknots of fronds are mainstays of any tropical and subtropical landscape. Most palms have huge inflorescences that attract many pollinators.

While many palms function as trees in the landscape, they are not true trees, botanically speaking, because they don't have a cambium layer under a coating of bark and they do not develop annual rings of wood like actual trees. Palms are monocots and are structured more like grasses. A cross-section of a palm trunk shows a curly or random fibrous grain rather than annual rings. This arrangement of woody tissue is usually quite flexible, making palms an excellent choice for wind-tolerant landscaping. Also, because there is no wood with expanding annual rings once a palm tree starts to grow vertically, its girth doesn't change much and its roots will not expand, either. Palms will not disturb landscape infrastructures such as sidewalks, foundations, or pavements, but do keep in mind that the fronds can get quite large. The other palm characteristic is that without bark and without a concentrated cambium layer, palms cannot heal wounds or gouges in their trunks, so if you have palms in your landscape, clear the area around them so that lawn mowers and string trimmers never come into contact with the trunks. Also, don't allow anyone to climb them using spikes on their boots.

After a palm seed sprouts, the plant goes into its establishment phase, when it looks and behaves like a shrubby palmetto, for at least several years depending upon species and conditions. This time is necessary for the development of its growing tip (the apical meristem), and for the establishment of the palm's girth prior to its vertical growth. Once its trunk is established, then the palm starts growing vertically, and all

The flowering fronds of cabbage palm (*Sabal palmetto*), with their thousands of fragrant flowers, are more than six feet long. They attract a good variety of pollinators.

the fronds and inflorescences are produced by the apical meristem, which will always be at the top of the tree. So if you chop off the top of a single-stemmed palm, it will die. Nonetheless, the cabbage palm got its name because people harvested the apical meristem (or the heart of palm) to eat in dishes similar to cabbage, but chopping off its top kills the tree. By the way, the heart of palm commonly available as a vegetable is usually harvested from fast-growing, multistemmed palms—usually a peach palm (*Bactris gasipaes*), native to South America—for a more sustainable crop.

Because they take so long to get started, almost all of the cabbage palms used for landscape plantings are transplants from the wild. When you see truckloads of cabbage palms, they have proportionally small root balls for the size of the trees, and they have most of their fronds trimmed off. This way, the trees do not have to support a full complement of fronds while they are trying to grow all new roots. Those new roots will develop from the root initiation zone at the bottom of the trunk. This is why palms usually are staked for six months or more when planted. Until new fronds start to grow, a newly planted palm tree will need additional water beyond the general landscape irrigation. After they are established, most palms are quite drought tolerant.

At no other time should a palm have its fronds tightly trimmed: once it's established in your landscape, it's best not to trim any of the fronds. If you feel the need to do so, only trim the dead fronds—never the green ones.

Palm versus Palmetto

Palmettos are common in Florida as understory shrubs. Our most common one is the saw palmetto (*Serenoa repens*), but there are a few others. The scientific name of the cabbage palm, which includes the term "palmetto" as the species epithet, confuses the issue of palm versus palmetto. Generally, a palmetto is a shrubby plant. The trunk of a mature palmetto isn't usually vertical for more than a few feet. The fibrous palmetto trunk grows either underground or it lies on top of the soil, while palms eventually develop vertical trunks. While a palm tree will look much like a palmetto while it develops its girth and a trunk, you can still identify whether it's a palmetto or a palm by the shape of the fronds and how they are attached to their stems.

Choosing Palms

Do some research before you purchase palms, to ensure that you select those that suit your climate and specific growing conditions in your landscape, such as sun exposure, salt spray, and soil moisture. Our native cabbage palm is usually the best choice in North and Central Florida, but there are several other palms native to South Florida. Be sure to avoid the queen palm (*Syagrus romanzoffiana*), even though it's widely available, because it's not wind tolerant like most other palms, and cold snaps will kill back much of its foliage when planted in North Florida. Plus, queen palms are also Category II invasives in Central and South Florida.

There are a number of non-native palms that are widely planted in Florida, but maybe the coconut palm has the most interesting history. On January 9, 1878, the Spanish brig *Providencia* was en route from Cuba to Spain, but the ship wrecked off the shores of Florida. Its cargo of 20,000 coconuts was scattered along the coast. The settlers of Florida took advantage of this accidental bounty and planted most of the stranded coconuts in their yards and along streets. The palms that grew from those coconuts gave Palm Beach County its name, and if you visit, there are still many coconut palms (*Cocos nucifera*) planted there today. Unfortunately, this palm is now on the Category II list of invasive plants in South Florida.

So plant some noninvasive palms in your landscape for some coarse texture and to create a tropical feel. It's best to choose species that are native to your region. Water them liberally while they become established, trim away only the dead fronds, and you'll find that palms and palmettos are wonderful drought-tolerant and wind-resistant additions to your yard.

Florida's Pines

There are seven pines native to Florida: sand pine (*Pinus clausa*), shortleaf pine (*P. echinata*), slash pine (*P. elliottii*), spruce pine (*P. glabra*), longleaf pine (*P. palustris*), pond pine (*P. serotina*), and loblolly pine (*P. taeda*). Most of the pines occur just in North Florida and north Central Florida, but the slash pine occurs in all of Florida, even into the Keys, where it plays a vital role in the pine rocklands plant communities. I'm sure you're familiar with pines in general, but the one I find most interesting is the longleaf pine. It's different in a number of ways. Longleaf pine once dominated the coastal plain of the southeastern United States, but today, only about 3 percent of the original community exists. Florida has most of the high-quality longleaf pine forests that remain and almost all of the old-growth forests. It dominates the high-pine plant community that is subjected to natural fires every few years.

Longleaf pines have evolved various ways to better tolerate frequent

Right: Several young longleaf pines (*Pinus palustris*) growing in an open, sandy forest are five to eight feet tall. These are in the bottle-brush stage because there are no side branches yet.

Below: A young longleaf pine grew on our septic drain field for more than a year. Because it was in the grassy stage, I at first thought it was a grass or a rush. It had to be moved. It was slow to adjust and recover after its transplant, but ten years later it was eight feet tall.

fires. Unlike other pines, they start out with a grassy stage for five to eight years as they develop a deep root system. If a fire passes during this stage, they only lose that year's needles and can easily start growing again. Once they start growing vertically, they grow quickly (up to five feet a year!) and do not put out any side branches for a year or two. This is called the bottlebrush stage. Again, if fire passes through, they lose only topknots of needles, and they don't provide much ladder fuel for the fire to climb higher. Their buds are covered with a dense layer of white hair, and their bark is thick. When they finally produce side branches, they are shorter than branches of other pines and point upward. Most other pine saplings grow into a pyramid shape, like Christmas trees, with broad, horizontal lower branches.

A longleaf pine forest that has experienced periodic ground fires will have a lovely parklike feeling with a wealth of interesting undergrowth, including some endemic plants that would be crowded out in a weedier, unburned environment. This ecosystem is important for many species of Florida's wildlife including the endangered Red-Cockaded Woodpecker (*Dryobates borealis*), which excavates cavities exclusively in living pine trees—mostly mature longleaf pines.

These pines are easy to recognize as young trees because of their unique growth habit, but the mature trees can be identified because of their clusters of three or four long needles, which are eight to eighteen inches long, and their large pinecones, which are seven to ten inches long. They are a good drought-tolerant choice for urban landscapes because of their fast growth and their narrow habit. Also, their extensive root systems provide more wind-resistance than other pines. If you have a sandy, sunny spot on your property with enough space for their hundred-foot height and deep roots, plant a grouping of these interesting native pines.

FLORIDA'S OAKS

There are twenty-six oaks (*Quercus* spp.) native to Florida. They are members of the beech family (Fagaceae). There are two sections of this genus. The first group is the red oaks; these often have sharp points on the lobes of their leaves and sometimes bristles at the ends of the lobes. Also, their acorns take two years to mature, so red oak acorns are extremely bitter because of the buildup of tannins over the long development time. The second group is the white oaks; these have rounded lobes on their leaves, or at least no sharp points or bristles, and their acorns mature in only one year, making them sweeter. White oaks are what you should choose if you're planning to forage acorns.

Most species of oaks occur in the more northern regions of the state, but there are a few that are native to the whole state. The oaks range in size from our huge, iconic southern live oak (*Q. virginiana*) to the dwarf live oak (*Q. minima*) that serves as a ground cover—and everything in between. Even though dwarf live oak is only six inches tall, it still plays a significant role in the native ecosystems, and its acorns are an important food source for Florida's only endemic bird, the Florida Scrub-Jay (*Aphelocoma coerulescens*).

The live oak is native to all of Florida and to southeastern states from Virginia to Texas. It's in the white oak section and can grow to fifty feet or more in height and eighty feet or more wide, so this tree is not for the small yard. The sand live oak (*Q. geminata*) is somewhat smaller and is more suitable for smaller landscapes.

Once established, southern live oak is drought tolerant and wind tolerant. Because it's so large, it creates lots of highly desirable shade for your yard, and with all those leaves, the transpiration rate is extremely high, which means that a live oak will significantly cool the air. Don't try to have a lawn under this tree. Instead, plant ferns, shade-tolerant bunching grasses or ground covers, and acid-loving understory shrubs, which will vary depending upon your planting zone. Live oak's wide, horizontal branches provide good habitat for plants and animals.

Florida's Hollies

There are fourteen hollies, both trees and shrubs, that are native to Florida—mostly in North Florida and northern Central Florida. American holly (*Ilex opaca*) is probably familiar to you since it's native to most of eastern North America, including North Florida. Some hollies, like winterberry (*I. verticillata*), which is native to most of the southeastern states including North Florida, are deciduous and

What's Growing on Your Oak?

Oaks, particularly live oaks, have broad, nearly horizontal branches that host a number of other plants and lichens. Most are epiphytes, or air plants, that do no harm to your tree, because they gain their water and nutrients from the air. Mistletoe, however, is a partial parasite. Either way, these plants do not need to be removed for "the health of your tree."

Lichens are three organisms—a fungus, an alga, and a bacterium—living together in a symbiotic relationship. They are epiphytes and occur on rocks, soil, trees, and shrubs. They tend to grow more thickly on dead branches, and some people may suppose that the lichens caused the twig to die; instead, however, the lichens are only taking advantage of good light in places where leaves have been disappearing above. Lichen spores germinate and survive in greater numbers on increasingly bare twigs and branches. They are not the cause of the decline and death.

Epiphytic members of the bromeliad family (Bromeliaceae) include various species of *Tillandsia,* which include ball moss (*T. recurvata*), cardinal airplant (*T. fasciculata*), Bartram's airplant (*T. bartramii*), and other air plant species. The most famous and iconic of this genus is Spanish moss (*T. usneoides*). Yes, this means that it's a flowering plant, not a moss. Also, it's native to this hemisphere—in mostly coastal regions from southern Maryland south to South America—so it's not Spanish. The native Americans called it *itla-okla,* or tree hair, and when they communicated this to the early French explorers, who were in a type of competition with the Spanish explorers, the French named it *barbe Espagñol,* or Spaniard's beard. The Spanish explorers then called it *cabello Francés,* or French hair. The French name was modified to Spanish moss, and that stuck in our lexicon.

Epiphytic orchids (Orchidaceae) are often found on spreading oak branches, but they mostly occur in the southern coastal regions of the state. The most famous of these orchids is the rare ghost orchid (*Dendrophylax lindenii*), which is found in southwestern Florida. You're more likely to see the Florida butterfly orchid (*Encyclia tampensis*), which is native to South and Central Florida.

Resurrection fern (*Pleopeltis polypodioides*) is a true fern that reproduces via spores, but it is also an epiphyte. The common name of resurrection fern is due to its ability to lose up to 95 percent of its moisture, stop its

(continued)

photosynthesis, and go into a type of suspended state; it appears to be dead. When it rains, or when the humidity becomes high enough, the fronds unfurl and turn green in a matter of hours. Hence the name resurrection fern—it arises from the dead.

American or eastern mistletoe (*Phoradendron leucarpum*) is a shrublet native to the whole southeastern section of the United States, from New Jersey to Florida; it occurs on all the oaks and on other trees as well. It is a partial parasite (a hemiparasite, to use the botanical term), because it has green leaves and produces its own sugar through photosynthesis. But to survive, it must grow from the branches of a host tree, using special rootlike projections called haustoria, which invade the host tree to extract moisture and whatever nutrients are in the tree's system. You can estimate the age of a mistletoe plant by the number of branch divisions. Count the number of forks in a single branch to its end and then add two to that number for the age. It takes a year for the haustoria to invade the host and develop its network of cells to accept the fluids; the second year, it sprouts without any branches. When you see the size of some of the mistletoe globes, many are probably more than fifty years old.

Mistletoe needs birds. The seeds are very sticky (hence the family name Viscaceae for "viscous"), and as birds eat the fruit, the seeds stick to their beaks, which they wipe onto the tree bark, where it sticks. Alternatively, the seeds are swallowed along with the fruit and are later deposited on a branch by birds with a dollop of fertilizer.

And birds need mistletoe. Foresters used to consider mistletoe to be a pest plant that ruins trees, but it's been shown that the mistletoes play an important role in forest ecosystems, and trees actually do better where mistletoes are present. Birds, especially migratory birds, depend on mistletoe berries, which are available in an off-season from most other plants. Insects and other soil critters depend upon the nutrients found in the fleshy leaves that drop on a year-round basis. When researchers considered all the studies, they determined that mistletoes are a keystone species in their ecosystems.

For more information on the ecological importance of mistletoe, see David M. Watson and Matthew Herring's 2012 article "Mistletoe as a Keystone Resource," https://royalsocietypublishing.org/doi/10.1098/rspb.2012.0856.

lose their leaves in the winter, leaving only berries on the branches in winter. But most hollies are evergreen and keep their leaves through the winter and thus serve as important winter shelter for birds and other wildlife. Hollies are dioecious, with individual plants bearing either male flowers or female flowers, but not both. Only the female plants bear the berries. (Actually, the fruit is a drupe and not a true berry, but let's not split these botanical hairs.)

One of Florida's native hollies is a naturally occurring hybrid— called the East Palatka holly (*I. × attenuata*)—which is a cross between dahoon holly (*I. cassine*) and American holly (*I. opaca*). It is widely sold because the female trees carry a heavy load of berries. The holly with the widest distribution in Florida is inkberry (*I. glabra*), an understory shrub that's three to seven feet tall with, as you might have guessed, black berries. It's native to all of Florida except for the Keys. The hollies do best in somewhat acidic soil paired with pines, magnolias, and the like.

I think the yaupon holly (*I. vomitoria*) may be the most interesting Florida holly, for several reasons. Its native range includes the coastal regions from North Carolina to eastern Texas and includes North and Central Florida. This plant was traditionally used by indigenous peoples to make a caffeinated drink with almost the same strength as today's coffee. It's thought to be the only plant native to North America that produces caffeine. The species epithet, *vomitoria,* was assigned by Europeans who incorrectly thought that the tea from this plant caused vomiting.

Yaupon holly grows from ten to twenty-five feet tall and is widely used in Florida landscaping. It's drought tolerant, somewhat salt-spray tolerant, and produces suckers to fill in an area for good screening. There are a number of cultivars, from a weeping form to compact shrubs. And this brings us to the next topic, shrubs.

Shrubs

The demarcation line between trees and shrubs is a bit hazy. Tall shrubs can play the role of trees, especially in small yards or in tight spaces. And small trees can serve as shrubs, especially in hedgerows or in understory plantings that serve as screening. Most people use fifteen to twenty feet as the general dividing line between trees and shrubs.

When we moved into our house, there were small, globular evergreen shrubs (about fifteen inches in all directions) planted in the front of the house. With these shrubs, the two magnolias in the lawn, and the roses in the back bed, the former owner had set up a version of the default Florida home landscape, even though the lot had been forested before the house and septic system had been installed—an extensive lawn, foundation shrubs, and some lawn trees.

WHY ARE FOUNDATION SHRUBS UBIQUITOUS?

The prevalence of foundation shrubs is not just in Florida; it is again a holdover from the formal gardens of Europe and the British Isles, with their boxwood hedges. This is what is expected and is easy to implement for the developers. A tidy row of shrubs hiding the foundation is part of the "curb appeal" for urban and suburban houses. There is a whole industry of growers raising cute shrubs to supply the demand.

But . . . there are significant problems with woody plants placed so close to the house, and most of these problems are due to shrubs, even dwarf or spreading shrubs, outgrowing the narrow spaces next to the house. We've all seen houses with overgrown shrubs hiding the windows and spreading out over the sidewalks. Here are some more specific problems:

* They require regular trimming as they age to keep them from outgrowing their space, and because most plants do not tolerate severe trimming year after year, the shrubs may die back.
* Because the default design is that all the shrubs would be the same species, if there is a blight or infestation of some type on that shrub, the whole landscape along the foundation will be affected.
* The constant moisture around the shrubs right next to the house will encourage algae and mold to grow on the house.
* Having woody plants so close to the house makes it difficult to do house maintenance, such as pressure washing, painting, or termite treatments.

* Overgrown shrubs could be a security risk, giving would-be thieves places to hide.
* Because shrubs are woody plants, their roots expand each year, and while not as aggressive as full-sized trees, shrubs could damage the foundation or sidewalks as the shrubs age.

The foundation shrubs planted in front of our house were evergreen with small oblong leaves. They had tiny white blooms in the spring, but no fruit. They served as a boxwood look-alike, but without the cat-urine odor. I eventually figured out that they were a dwarf, male-clone cultivar of our native yaupon holly (*Ilex vomitoria*). Even though they were a dwarf variety, they still grew way too large for the space between the front porch and the sidewalk. Dean added a hedge trimmer to his collection of battery-powered tools to keep them at four feet tall and wide. After several years of this shearing, the die-back began. We trimmed away the dead branches thinking that more light would help them grow back, but after more than a year, it was clear they would not. Dean got out the battery-powered chainsaw and cut them back to eighteen inches all around, and they did start growing back from there. He says he's going to keep them small. The other characteristic of yaupon holly is that it spreads via underground runners, which also makes it questionable as a choice for narrow spaces next to foundations.

Alternative Foundation Plantings

Use herbaceous plants such as bunching grasses, native ferns, a pollinator garden, a cottage garden, or an herb garden. In our back beds next to the house, we pulled out the roses and now use most of that bed for vegetables. Once you stop thinking that shrubs are necessary, your list of alternatives grows. Do keep in mind how much sun each bed receives and plant accordingly.

Shrubs Are Versatile

Shrubs have a wide variety of uses:

* They can be understory plants for groupings of trees and at edges of wooded areas. It's been shown that when shrubs and herbaceous plants form a buffer area at the edges of wooded areas, the habitat values are much higher than when those plant groupings are not adjoining.
* They can provide screening—not only for blocking a view, but also to lessen noise, dust, and salt spray.
* In tight bunches, they provide good wildlife habitat.
* They can be part of rain-garden plantings to absorb more water than herbaceous plants. (More information on this in the chapter on stormwater management.)

When using shrubs as a screen, think about building a hedgerow using different species that have different seasonal interests and different forms. Plant them in a zigzag pattern and far enough apart so each shrub can fill out to its own form. This will be more sustainable and easier to maintain than tightly trimmed hedges.

Four Recommended Shrubs for Florida

We have many excellent choices for native shrubs to use in our Florida landscapes. Here are four good-looking shrubs that are easy to find at native nurseries, not fussy about soil, able to grow in sunny or shady locations, and easy to care for.

1. **Beautyberry** (*Callicarpa americana*), a member of the mint family (Lamiaceae), is native to all of Florida and to most southeastern states. It's deciduous, so in the winter the branches are bare except for its incredibly luminous purple berries. It has gracefully arching branches and can grow to eight feet tall and as wide, but in South Florida it's a bit smaller. It has berries in the fall through the winter that feed the birds and can also be used for jellies or breads. It will self-seed to some extent.

2. **Southern wax myrtle** (*Morella cerifera;* formerly *Myrica cerifera*), a member of the wax myrtle family (Myricaceae), is an evergreen tall shrub or small tree up to eighteen feet tall that produces berries that are an important food source for migrating birds in the winter. It's dioecious, so you'll need both male and female shrubs to produce berries. It fixes nitrogen in the soil at twice the rate of legumes, so it can grow well in poor soils—both damp and dry. It tends to send up sprouts once established, so it makes a good thick screening plant, but do keep this trait in mind when selecting a location. If necessary, it tolerates regular trimming. The fragrant wax around the berries was used to make bayberry candles, although its relative, northern bayberry (*Morella pensylvanica*), was preferred for candle making.

3. **Simpson's stopper** (*Myrcianthes fragrans*), a member of the myrtle family (Myrtaceae), is an evergreen tall shrub or small tree up to eighteen feet tall and nearly as wide. It produces masses of fragrant white flowers and showy red-orange berries. It's an important pollinator and bird food plant. It's native to all of South Florida and along the Atlantic Coast as far north as St. Augustine.

The beautyberry (*Callicarpa americana*) lives up to its name with its iridescent purple fruit. The birds like it as well. In this photo (taken in our yard), there's a Gray Catbird in the upper right corner and a Northern Cardinal in the lower left corner.

It does best in drier habitats. It will become more treelike in shadier locations and more of a shrub in full sun.

4. **Coontie** (*Zamia integrifolia*) is a slow-growing, long-lived cycad that is native to all but the northernmost regions of the state. Cycads are an ancestral group of nonflowering plants and are dioecious, so there are separate male and female plants. It has no wood, so it's technically not a shrub, but it plays that role in the landscape and it will never get too tall for the landscape. It's drought tolerant and can grow in full sun or slight shade. Despite its general toxicity to humans (and dogs and cats), the tuberous roots were processed by indigenous peoples and used as a source of starch. Indeed, "arrowroot" is its other common name. Also, for many years, this starch was used in the making of animal crackers, giving them that slightly slimy texture. It was harvested almost to extinction, which in turn almost caused the extinction of the Atala butterfly, or coontie hairstreak (*Eumaeus*

Coonties (*Zamia integrifolia*) are hardy, but slow-growing plants that provide a ferny texture in a low-growing hedge or as a specimen plant in a small space. They do best in sunny or mostly sunny locations.

atala), which requires this plant as its larval food source. After the harvesting stopped, the population recovered a bit, but what really put it back on the map is that commercial landscapers realized that these good-looking shrubs would not grow too tall and would not block visibility in parking lots.

Be aware that two other cycads typically used in Florida landscapes are non-natives: the cardboard palm (*Z. furfuracea*), which has a narrow native range in eastern Mexico, and the sago palm (*Cycas revoluta*), which is native to Japan.

Woody Plants Provide Many Benefits

Trees and shrubs are the most permanent and prominent landscape plants. Time spent planning for and choosing the most appropriate trees and shrubs for your landscape, and handling them carefully, will mean greater survival rates, fewer problems, and less work in the long run. Plus growing more trees and shrubs increases the value of your property, cools the air, and is good for the planet.

References

For more information on Florida's woody plants, visit the University of Florida's "Landscape Plants" website, at https://hort.ifas.ufl.edu/woody/.

For detailed planting information on Florida's natives, I recommend Gil Nelson's *Florida's Best Native Landscape Plants: 200 Readily Available Species for Homeowners and Professionals* (Gainesville: University Press of Florida, 2003).

6

◦⌣◦

Growing Food in Florida

Florida is a wonderful place to grow edibles. We can grow so many different food crops here, and edible gardening is possible on a year-round basis. But the timing of the seasons is really weird for gardeners transplanted here from more northerly climates. One of my early columns, "Tomatoes Are for Summer," showed that I hadn't really adjusted my thinking to the Florida climate. The title is misleading for Florida, because once the low nighttime temperatures are higher than 73°F, which is normal even in North Florida, most tomatoes stop setting fruit. And since summer is our wet season, some tomato varieties are prone to fungal wilt diseases. A better title would have been, "Don't Plant Tomatoes in the Summer in Florida." In North Florida, we plant tomatoes as early as possible in the spring and again in the late summer for a fall crop. In frost-free sections of South Florida, tomatoes are planted in the fall and grow through the winter. Ahh, the lessons learned.

Growing food in Florida is a huge topic, and people have written whole books about it, including me! The purpose of the discussion in this book is to highlight a few of our famous and not-so-famous crops and to provide tips on how to avoid some common pitfalls as you get started.

There are a number of crops that require longer or more reliable cold periods than what we experience in Florida, so you might have to skip some of your favorites, or at least find cultivars that are bred to withstand our warmer climate. Here's a partial list: rhubarb, most apples, parsnips, asparagus, artichoke, and Brussels sprouts. I know of a guy in Jacksonville who simulates winter with a daily coating of ice shavings from a local fish market for six weeks on his asparagus bed. I'm not that dedicated. On the other hand, we can grow a whole bunch of crops that would turn your northern friends green as avocados with envy. So my advice is to learn to love where you are instead of pining for what you used to grow somewhere else.

In 2019, the Florida legislature passed a law disallowing local municipalities from banning vegetable gardens on any part of a residential property. While it seems like a double-negative rule and it does not apply to HOAs, it is a step in the right direction because sometimes the best sun exposure is in the front yard, and more people should be growing their own vegetables and fruit for many reasons. The inspiration for this law was a lawsuit in Miami Shores where the city fined a couple for growing vegetables in their front yard. This was one of my topics when I spoke to the Clay County delegation in 2018. (Each year, in every county before the Florida legislative session, the state senators and representatives hold an open meeting to hear from local governments, organizations, and citizens.) In our county, private citizens have three minutes to make their cases. My senator agreed with my plea and wrote and sponsored a front-yard vegetable garden bill. The next year we had this law. Sometimes, it pays to speak out.

Having vegetable gardens in our yards harkens back to old Florida, when every settler's house had a vegetable garden, and to the Victory Gardens during World War II. I strongly believe that people should grow more of their own food, and here in Florida, we have a wonderful array of interesting crops to grow.

Raised Beds

First of all, and for several reasons, raised beds and intensive cropping are recommended for home gardeners and small farm operations for most nonwoody crops anywhere in Florida. We don't use tractors in our gardens, so we don't need those wide spaces between growing areas and we don't need to maintain them. Raised beds allow us to

I've been building raised beds without sides and have used wide-row planting for intensive, high-density plantings with the spacing between rows adjustable to suit the crop size. After planting, I mulch with pine needles both around the outside of the beds and in the trenches between the rows to keep the soil and moisture in place and to reduce weeds. In the background is a vigorous okra crop.

better control the soil and to focus the irrigation, enrichments, and maintenance to only the growing areas—not the spaces between the crops. Also, by our not stepping in the growing areas, the crop roots suffer less damage. In addition, by not plowing the soil each season and leaving the underlying soil intact, it reduces your labor, reduces the release of carbon dioxide, and supports the soil's ecosystem. The raised beds can be built with or without hard sides. Common materials for the sides are cinder blocks, lumber (not pressure-treated), fake lumber, or metal.

For years, I have maintained raised beds without hard sides, which I arrange in wide rows separated by trenches. This allows for better drainage and more flexibility in structuring the growing areas to suit the crops each season. I use an intensive growing system so crops are spaced for their optimum growth with little room for weeds. Plus, I vary the width of the trenches between the rows depending upon how much room the crops will need. It's similar to square-foot gardening, but without the constraints of the one-foot barriers. Also, I create a

Creating raised swales is useful for planting squash crops or other large moisture-loving crops like tomatoes and okra. Underneath the swale I lay in a good thick layer of dead leaves to hold the moisture. I plant the seeds (or seedlings in the case of tomatoes and peppers) around the edge of the swale. Before the seeds sprout or while the seedlings are still small, I'll often bury kitchen scraps in the center of the swale to increase water retention and nutrients. Once the plants are large enough, I hand irrigate into the swale only to concentrate the water. Rain and general landscape irrigation will also collect in the swale. This swale was for Seminole pumpkins, which get very large. If it had been for okra or tomatoes, I would have put a ridge across the center to form two swales and nine planting sites—three across the ridge and three on each end. The okra in the previous photo was planted in this way. Note the pine needles raked into a pile on the lawn—I reused them around the outside walls of the swale.

slight swale in the planting surface on the tops of these rows to allow water to soak in. After the seeds are planted, I firmly pat down both the tops and the sides of these rows to ensure soil contact with the seeds and to solidify the rows for the season.

After the rows are planted, I use pine needle mulch around the outside of the raised bed and in the trenches between the rows to hold in the soil and its moisture and to reduce the weeds. At the end of the growing season, I rake away the pine needles to use again for the next set of crops. Pine needles last two or more years before they decompose, and it's been shown that they do not significantly acidify the soil. In addition, they are free for me in our piney neighborhood—I rake them from our driveway and from the local streets, plus a neighbor, with many more pines in his yard than ours, delivers loads of needles to my pile.

Cool-Weather Crops

Fall, winter, and spring are the best seasons for growing edibles here. When we first moved here, I was surprised that we can grow cool-weather crops right through the winter, even here in northeastern Florida (Zone 9a) where we experience six to ten killing frosts from December through February. We can grow various cole crops such as cabbage, broccoli, and kale. We can also grow lettuces, spinach, Swiss chard, beets, carrots, radishes, onions, garlic, and sugar snap peas, which may lose their flowers in a hard frost but perk up again soon afterward. Various herbs such as parsley and dill are other cool-weather crops that grow here, and some Mediterranean perennial herbs such as rosemary, chives, garlic chives, and oregano last through our winters.

Cole Crops

There are many cole crops (cabbage, kale, collard greens, Brussels sprouts, broccoli, cauliflower, kohlrabi, and more), which have all been bred from just one plant species (*Brassica oleracea*) in the cabbage family (Brassicaceae). *Kohl* is the German word for cabbage—hence they are the "cole crops" and this is why cabbage salad is called coleslaw.

Most cole crops are easy to grow through Florida's winter months, but Brussels sprouts need a four-month-long cool season, and we don't usually have enough reliable cold for a good crop. Cauliflower is a bit frost sensitive and is usually best planted in midwinter so that it matures during a relatively frost-free time period. Also, it's traditionally grown with its leaves fastened together over the head to keep it pale. Kohlrabi is a bit weird in that we harvest its enlarged stem, which is sweet and crispy. The word *kohlrabi* means "cabbage turnip" in German, which seems appropriate because of the size of its stem enlargement.

Broccoli is probably our favorite cole crop. I leave the plants in place after I harvest the main curd or head. Then I harvest the side shoots as the plants try to produce flowers. Those smaller curds are sweeter because they are produced more quickly. This come-again broccoli harvest can continue for a couple of months as long as you keep harvesting. The blooms are edible as well, if you wait a bit too long to cut off the curds. In the end, the come-again broccoli harvest is likely to be a much larger volume than those big heads. Don't harvest the leaves during the come-again harvest time because the plant needs the energy to keep producing those new shoots. At the end of the season, though, you can harvest the leaves, which you could use as cabbage and the stems, which you can cube to use in soups or salads.

Onion Family

Some botanists put onions in their own family, Alliaceae, while others put them in the amaryllis family (Amaryllidaceae); these groups have also at times been placed in the lily family (Liliaceae). Regardless, our crop plants are in the *Allium* genus, which is divided botanically into two sections: the onions, which have hollow leaves, and the garlics, which have flat, solid leaves. All parts of the plants, from the bulbs to the flowers, are edible.

Onions

The bulbing onions (*Allium cepa*) are biennial plants. Their natural rhythm is to grow from a seed into a plant, and then into a dormant bulb in the first year. The following spring, the stored energy in the

A wide-row plantings of broccoli, onions, and carrots. These onions were almost ready to harvest when I took this photo because most of the leaves had fallen over. While onions do best with consistent moisture, when half of the leaves fall over, stop all irrigation to urge the plants into dormancy before the harvest.

bulb will produce a flower spike. We interrupt this natural cycle when we harvest them after the bulb is formed and when they are going dormant.

We grow onions through the winter here in Florida, so we can only grow short-day onions. Sometimes long-day onion varieties are sold to gardeners here, so pay attention to that because those would not form bulbs before the hot season ends the growing cycle. I've grown onions from sets and by seed, but now I order onion plants. I plant them in a grid pattern in my wide rows four inches apart. I usually plant sweet onions that are the same variety as Vidalia onions, but these sweet onions can only be marketed as Vidalias if they are grown in the four counties surrounding Vidalia, Georgia. Ours are just as sweet.

Onions do best with good moisture and rich soil. You should keep them weeded, but that task becomes less of a problem as the bulbs expand to fill the whole growing space. It's time to harvest them when most of the leaves fall over. Let the soil in the bed dry out, pull all the onions, and hang them by their leaves in a dry spot for a few weeks; this way, they will go into complete dormancy and store well.

Sometimes, here in Florida, a few of the onions bloom during the first year. Harvest these rogue onions as they go to flower and use them quickly since they don't store well. Even though the bulb is likely to be small because of the energy used to produce the flower scape, you can use the whole plant, except for the roots, in salads, stir-fries, or in soups.

Garlic

There are two major categories of garlic (*A. sativum*): the hard-neck, which is the one most often sold in grocery stores, and the soft-neck variety, which is what we need to successfully grow here in Florida. I plant the garlic cloves at the same time as I plant the onions since they both have a long winter growing cycle. I also use the same grid planting pattern of about four inches apart. FYI, elephant garlic is a type of leek (*A. ampeloprasum*), which we can grow in North and Central Florida.

Allium herbs

Chives (*A. schoenoprasum*) are perennials that are native to most of Europe and Asia. They are in the onion division of the alliums because they have hollow leaves. We can grow them here in North Florida, but they only last a few years, so I plant seeds every other year or so, to ensure a continuous crop.

Garlic chives (*A. tuberosum*) are a clump-forming perennial with small, tough bulbs. They are native to just a small area in Asia. The flat, strap-shaped leaves put it in the garlic side of the alliums, and it's the leaves that are used, not the bulbs. The leaves taste more like garlic than onion and are useful in salads, but since the leaves are solid, they are particularly useful cooked in soups, stews, and stir-fries. I'd never grown it before we moved to Florida, but it's an impressive and vigorous crop that provides a bountiful, year-round harvest. It has lasted for more than ten years and I've given lots of it away over the years.

Meadow garlic (*A. canadense*) is a perennial wild garlic that is native to all of eastern North America except for South Florida. It's about the

Meadow garlic (*Allium canadense*) produces flower heads that are a combination of stalked flowers and bulblets, which usually sprout while still attached to the plant giving it a wild-haired look. This habit gives the bulblets a better chance of survival, and indeed, this plant can become a bit weedy in your vegetable beds. We eat the weeds!

same size as chives, but it produces flat leaves and flower heads with both bulblets and white flowers on stalks. Years ago, I gathered some bulblets from a roadside ditch near my house one spring and invited this native into my gardens next to the chives. It has done amazingly well in my enriched beds. You can eat all parts of the plant, and it has a somewhat different flavor and texture than the others. It dies back after blooming in late spring and resprouts in late fall.

Perennial Crops

In my garden, I tend to group together the perennial crops such as alliums and other herbs like oregano and rosemary. This keeps them away from the hustle and bustle of the ever-changing seasonal crops and cover crops. I move them after several years so they have fresh enriched soil. Also, knowing where they are, if they die back like the meadow garlic, then I won't accidentally plant over them.

Warm-Weather Crops

Okay, first let me clarify. There are several categories or divisions of warm-weather crops based on their frost sensitivity and their heat and moisture tolerance in Florida:

* Crops that we cannot grow through the winter in North and Central Florida, but still require cool weather: We plant these in late January or early February. In South Florida, they'd be planted in late fall. This group includes cauliflower and Irish potatoes (*Solanum tuberosum*), which are native to South America, not Ireland.
* Warm-weather crops that do not tolerate our hot, wet summers: This group includes tomatoes, most members of the squash family, and some beans. In North and Central Florida, we plant these right after the danger of frost in early spring and maybe again in early fall for a second crop. In South Florida, you plant them in late fall.
* Crops that thrive in our hot, wet summers: This group includes peppers, eggplant, okra, sweet potato, and Seminole pumpkin. There are also spinach substitutes, such as Malabar spinach (*Basella alba*) and New Zealand spinach (*Tetragonia tetragonoides*), that can be grown through the summer.
* Tropical, long-lived crops that only grow in frost-free zones or in containers that can be moved inside during cold weather: Pineapple (*Ananas comosus*) is a good example of this group.

The Basils

The basils are popular and fragrant herbs in the mint family (Lamiaceae). They are tender annuals. The most frequently planted are sweet basil (*Ocimum basilicum*), lime basil (*O. americanum*) (which is native to Africa, India, and Asia, but not to the Americas, despite its species name), and lemon basil (*O. × africanum*), which is a hybrid between the sweet and lime basils. In addition, the wild sweet basil (*O. campechianum*), which is native to South Florida, Central America, and South America, has been gaining in popularity with its more minty fragrance and can be used like the others.

Sweet basil is susceptible to downy mildew in our hot, wet summers, so grow it early in the season. Lime basil and lemon basil thrive during our wet summers. I purchased lime basil seeds once, and because it grows so well, my harvests have not kept up with its growth, so it has reseeded itself. It's become part of our seed bank in the edible beds and germinates as a volunteer when I prepare wide rows for a crop. I plan for this, and in the spring, I leave an empty row for them and transplant them once they grow a few sets of true leaves. It has a bit of a citrus tang, but I've used it all the ways that I use sweet basil.

The Tomato Family

Actually, the more proper common name for this family is the nightshade family (Solanaceae); it includes several poisonous plants such as nightshade, or belladonna, and tobacco. But it also includes some of our favorite crops: tomatoes, potatoes, peppers, and eggplants.

Tomatoes (*Solanum lycopersicum*) are native to Peru. As I've mentioned previously, they are warm-weather plants, but they also need cool nights. When our low nighttime temperatures are higher than 73°F, most tomatoes stop setting fruit, but in general, cherry tomatoes are a bit more tolerant of the warm nights. Here in North Florida, we plant tomatoes as early as possible in the spring and maybe again in the fall. In South Florida, tomatoes are planted in the fall to grow through the winter. They do best with good moisture, but not on their leaves, and to reduce fungal infections, don't touch the tomato plants when the leaves are wet. They also don't tolerate soggy roots, so I use the swale method of planting. I plant two or three seedlings positioned around a small swale and then direct them to grow inside a five-foot-tall wire tomato cage. When hand irrigating, I direct the water into the swales, never on the plants. The Everglades tomato or currant tomato (*S. pimpinellifolium*), a tiny orange cherry tomato, does produce even in the summers. It has escaped in South Florida, but it's native to South America. Tomatoes are susceptible to several diseases. You will probably have the best success if you purchase cultivars tagged with the letters VFN. This indicates that they are resistant to verticillium wilt, fusarium wilt, and nematodes.

Potatoes (*S. tuberosum*) are a frost-sensitive, cool-weather crop. Even though it's sometimes called an Irish potato, this species is native to western South America. The common advice is to plant only certified seed potatoes (not real seeds from the flowers, but chunks of potatoes with three or more eyes, or embryonic plants), but by the time standard producers from farther north are ready to start shipping, it's likely to be March, which is much too late for us. I've had the best luck with growing potatoes from the grocery store purchased in November or December that I let sit in the pantry until they begin to sprout. That way I can get them into my potato trenches by the end of January. I protect them from frost by burying all but their topmost leaves with loose soil. In South Florida, you'd back it up by a couple of months. Be careful not to let the potato tubers be exposed to the light while they are growing, because if they turn green, they'll contain toxic alkaloids.

Eggplant (*S. melongena*) is a warm-weather crop native to India and southeastern Asia. Plants may be available as seedlings for sale, but planting seeds will allow for the widest selection of cultivars. Plant those seeds into flats or pots six weeks before your garden planting date. They will grow through the summer. Harvest the fruit while the skin is still glossy for the best results.

Peppers (*Capsicum annuum*) are mostly native to Mexico, and in the wild, they can be hot or not. Early peoples bred them to control the spiciness. Peppers grow well through our summers. They can get rangy, so I usually grow them in groups of three or four in a wire tomato cage. Our native bird pepper (*C. annuum* var. *glabriusculum*) is spicy and has become quite popular to add diversity in the pepper crops.

THE SQUASH FAMILY

Members of the squash family (Cucurbitaceae) are usually vines that can be trellised or allowed to crawl. Each vine will bear separate male and female flowers. The usual growing habit is for a vine to produce bunches of male flowers first before it produces the females. It's a good idea to have a pollinator garden nearby so there is a readily available supply of pollinators. Each female flower must be pollinated seven to ten times for its fruit to develop. If not pollinated, the small fruit at the base of the flower will not expand; it will just turn yellow and drop off the vine. If I see an obviously unpollinated fruit, I harvest it quickly before it falls off, slice it into little disks and add to salads or soups.

This family includes a few different genera of crop plants that we can grow in Florida. Most are susceptible to fungal wilts in our hot, wet summers and should be harvested before summer or planted in the fall. Your squash-planting strategies will vary depending upon your location in Florida.

Squashes and pumpkins (*Cucurbita* spp.) are divided into two groups. First are the summer squashes, which are harvested while green. They have a soft skin and are used right after harvest, such as summer squash and zucchinis. The other group comprises the winter squashes, which have a thicker skin and are allowed to ripen in the field. They can be stored for months into the winter. This group includes the pumpkins, spaghetti squash, butternut squash, Seminole pumpkins, and some of the gourds.

Watermelons (*Citrullus* spp.) include several species, with *C. lanatus* being the most prominent.

Melons (*Cucumis* spp.) include cucumbers (*C. sativus*) as well as muskmelons, cantaloupes, and honeydews (*C. melo*).

Chayote, or christophene (*Sechium edule*), a remarkable squash family member native to Central America, is in its own group. Chayote is a tender perennial that comes back after frosts in North Florida, if it's heavily mulched over in the winter, but in frost-free zones in South Florida, it can produce continuously. Unlike other plants in this family, the fruit has one large seed. You can buy it in some specialty grocery stores or farmers markets. To plant it, let the fruit sit on a counter until it sprouts, then plant the whole fruit, with the sprouted end above the soil surface, in the garden near a sturdy trellis. Once established, one vine might produce more than a hundred fruits annually. When you cook it, it's similar to a yellow summer squash, but if it's not cooked, it's a bit crisp. It's used raw in salsas and the like. The new growth at the ends of the vines is also edible and tasty. These tender stem tips can be prepared like asparagus.

The Seminole pumpkin (*Cucurbita moschata*) is my favorite. It does well in our hot, wet summers after the others have faded. It's native to Mexico, but it was traded by indigenous peoples and was being grown in Florida when the Spaniards first arrived five hundred years ago. The butternut squash is a cultivar of this species. Because it thrives in the summer, I usually plant it in April or May as the cool-weather crops

The Seminole pumpkin (*Cucurbita moschata*) produces a bountiful harvest and can bear several different shaped fruits. It's so vigorous that if you stand too close, it will try to wrap itself around your ankle!

are fading. The fruits vary in size and shape. They can be a flattened pumpkin, have a long neck with bulbous bottom, or have a teardrop shape. It can be harvested while green or after it ripens. Its thick skin is generally resistant to caterpillars or pickle worms that bore into squash fruits. Its large flowers are edible either raw in salads or stuffed with cheese and fried. Plan for a large space for this crop. I usually surround it with temporary wire fencing to keep it in check. It grows six or more inches a day, and I documented a female flower that grew to a foot-long fruit in just six days.

PINEAPPLE

Pineapple (*Ananas comosus*) is a tropical plant native to South America in the bromeliad family (Bromeliaceae). *Pineapple* was a seventeenth-century English word for what we now call a pinecone. When early European explorers first saw this tropical fruit during that time, they called them "pineapples" because of their resemblance to pinecones. Of course, this fruit has nothing to do with apples or pines. In most of the world, the fruit is known by its genus name, *Ananas,* which is derived from the word the Tupi people of Brazil used for "excellent fruit."

You can use pineapple tops to start plants. Cut one inch below the very top and let it air-dry for a few days. You may plant the top directly into the garden in frost-free areas or into a container. Plant in rich soil so only the spiky top is sticking out. It will need frequent irrigation until it becomes established, but not so much that it becomes soggy. Well-drained soil is best.

Some growers stake the shoot to keep it upright and to keep the fruit clean. Once the flower head forms, some growers also fashion wire cages attached to the stake and surrounding the fruit to keep squirrels and other critters at bay. Harvest it when the bottom starts to change from green to yellow. If you're growing it in the ground, the plant will produce new flower heads for several years.

The Mallow Family

The mallow or hibiscus family (Malvaceae) includes many of our favorite ornamental plants and a few crop plants, including okra, jute, cotton, and the so-called Florida cranberry. Florida also has many truly native plants in this family, including mallows, rosemallows, and wild cotton. The flowers are edible in all the plants in this family, as long as they have not been poisoned.

Okra (*Abelmoschus esculentus*) is native to India and grows well in Florida's hot, wet summers. Although these plants like lots of moisture, they also need well-drained soil. I use swales for planting them, and I usually place a series of wire tomato cages over the planting spots in the swale grid to keep them upright. If you provide good, rich soil and plenty of water, okra responds with exuberance. One year, my okra

Beautiful okra (*Abelmoschus esculentus*) flowers are loved by loved by pollinators and gardeners alike. You can see why this traditional southern crop is in the hibiscus family.

plants grew to nearly twenty feet tall. We had to use a stepladder to harvest the fruit.

Harvest early and often, because older fruit tends to be woody, and if the fruit is allowed to ripen on the plant, it will slow the production of new flowers. This is a bountiful crop, and just ten or twelve plants produce more than Dean and I can consume during the season, so we cut them into half-inch wheels and freeze them for use in the winter. Dean makes a mean pot of shrimp gumbo with our okra, which is a hearty and tasty winter dish.

Florida cranberry, or **roselle** (*Hibiscus sabdariffa*), is an annual fruiting hibiscus that is native to tropical Africa. It's planted in the spring in full sun, but it won't begin to bloom until after the fall equinox, so it's a fall crop. This is an unusual crop because we use the flower calyxes (that is, the fleshy sepals). It has a crisp apple-like texture and a tart cranberry-like flavor. When brewed as a tea, it has a beautiful bright red color. It can be used for jams or sauces, which could serve as a substitute for cranberry sauce. It has a rich history as an original homesteaders' plant yielding many pounds of highly nutritious and delicious sepals. It's easy to grow and is drought tolerant and disease resistant.

Cover Crops and Solarization

Once the wet season and hot weather arrives in June, many of our traditional crops will stop performing well, so Florida gardeners can take this opportunity to recondition the soil in our raised beds by composting in place. Or, if you've had problems with root-knot nematodes, University of Florida research shows that a cover crop of French marigolds (*Tagetes patula*) that is turned into the soil a couple of weeks before you're ready to plant your cool-weather crops effectively reduces the nematodes.

Another treatment for root-knot nematodes, weeds, and more is to solarize your edible beds for six weeks in the summer. You do this by clearing everything from the soil and irrigating it so that it's damp, laying a clear plastic sheet over the bed, and securing all the edges with soil and rocks or bricks so a windy storm can't move it. Time these treatments to end just as you'll be getting ready to grow your fall crops.

Florida's Fruits and Nuts

Florida is famous for its many woody fruit and nut crops; indeed, the variety of tropical fruit crops grown in the southern parts of the state is amazing. This is a lot for newcomers to take in, and it's too large a topic to cover fully here, so I'll just skim the surface to provide some background and warnings for crops that may be threatened with deadly diseases.

Citrus Crops

Florida is famous for its amazing citrus crops; for many decades, it was the top exporter of citrus in the world market, although now Brazil is the top producer. Citrus was so iconic that the state flower is the orange blossom, and much of Florida's tourism and other marketing through most of the twentieth century featured Florida's citrus crops. (The state *wildflower* is coreopsis, though.)

Citrus crops are mostly in the *Citrus* genus, but there are a few others. All are in the rue family (Rutaceae) and probably originated in Australia, China, or both. Most citrus is grown in frost-free areas of the state, but there are several cultivars and crops that can be grown in North Florida. Many of the citrus crops are hybrids and crosses, and many are grown on grafted rootstock. Some of our neighbors have citrus trees, and we have enjoyed some of their excess fruit over the years. If you end up with citrus in your yard, you should know that unlike any other woody crop, no mulch is used around the bottoms of those trees or shrubs. Keep the area weeded, and most of the time, you'll have just bare soil surrounding them.

There are problems in our citrus paradise, however, and recently even in our own North Florida neighborhood. Citrus greening is an incurable bacterial disease that can affect any citrus crop. It's carried by the Asian citrus psyllid (*Diaphorina citri*), a sucking insect that was

Are Citrus GMOs in Our Future?

While some cultivars and some species may be or become more resistant to citrus greening, it's my opinion that in the future, most citrus grown in Florida will have a built-in defense against the greening disease bacteria through GMO technology. This has happened before; for instance, more than twenty years ago, a virus carried by an insect devastated the papaya crop on most of the Hawaiian Islands. A GMO crop was developed that prevented the disease. Since then, most of the Hawaiian papayas are GMOs, and there have been zero ill effects for two decades.

I'm not going to delve too deeply into this complex and controversial topic, but here is a quick summary: GMOs have gotten a bad rap from those such as Roundup Ready crops, which allow farmers to spray their fields with that herbicide without killing the crop plants, which are genetically modified to survive the herbicide treatment. This has had some consequences. Tiny amounts of the herbicide have ended up in our food. Also, the widespread spraying has been killing the formerly abundant milkweeds (and many other wildflowers) around the fields that used to feed the migrating monarch butterflies, which are declining. But farmers often use Roundup to kill plants in the fields to get ready for the next crop without having to plow, and this no-till farming has become the norm for better soil health and to control soil erosion. Also, Roundup is sometimes used to kill non-GMO crops, such as wheat, so that it will dry better. So even if Roundup Ready GMO crops were banned, that weed killer may still end up in our food by other means.

GMOs allow commercial agriculture to operate more efficiently, and they are common in our food supply. Have you ever wondered what the heck canola is? That cooking oil is made from a GMO mustard seed grown in Canada—"Canada oil" became *canola*. There is a GMO rice crop that adds more beta carotene in the grain to make it more nutritious, which is important for poor people where rice is the dominant food. There are many other examples of beneficial GMOs, but it's common to find people and organizations that condemn all GMOs as evil. As our population grows, they are probably going to become more common, not less. On the other hand, at this point, certified organic growers do not use GMOs of any type.

first found in Florida in 1998 and has spread across the state since then. For current information on symptoms of this disease and what to do about it, consult your local Florida Agriculture Extension Service or their website, https://edis.ifas.ufl.edu.

Florida's Blueberries

Blueberries (*Vaccinium* spp.) are members of the heath family (Ericaceae). New Jersey is famous for blueberries, but here in Florida, we can't grow Jersey berries. We have a different group of blueberries to grow in Florida. All are varieties of different highbush species: highbush blueberry (*V. corymbosum*), rabbiteye blueberry (*V. virgatum*), farkleberry (*V. arboreum*), deerberry (*V. stamineum*), and several others; some are edible, but all are recommended as wildlife habitat. All of these *Vaccinium* shrubs grow best in acidic soil.

The blueberries bred for Florida crops are mostly crosses of rabbiteye blueberry and southern-adapted highbush blueberry. Blueberries are easy to grow organically because they have so few pests other than birds.

In 2009, I ordered three varieties bred for Florida: star, jewel, and emerald. They were developed at the University of Florida for our climate. As recommended, I bought three different cultivars to ensure good crossbreeding and pollination. I also have some wild deerberries growing at the edges of our wooded areas, so they probably add to that mix. When they were delivered during the first week in February, they were already blooming! For that first year, I removed the blooms so the plants would spend their energy on developing their roots and adjusting to their new home.

The growing instructions included with the plants said to protect them from late-winter freezes, lest the crop be damaged since they bloom so early. I planted them near the west-facing wall of the garage where it's warmer, but I never protected them from frosts; a number of years later, I moved them out to the middle of the backyard where the butterfly mound was, and there has never been a problem with frost damage.

We love our blueberry harvests, and yes, sometimes we share them with the birds. I have rooted some of the trimmings so there will be more for all of us.

Blueberries need rich, acidic soil. Our soil is already somewhat acidic with its overstory of pines and magnolias. I've mulched them heavily with pine needles and wood chips over the years. Don't use manure to enrich the soil, because it's generally alkaline. Blueberries are drought-tolerant shrubs, but they need supplemental irrigation for optimum berry production. This is especially true here in Florida, because flowering and berry production occurs during our dry season. After a few years, our blueberry shrubs grew to be six feet tall; we have enjoyed ample harvests over the years.

Avocados

In frost-free zones of Florida, avocados (*Persea americana*) are an important crop. They are in the laurel family (Lauraceae) and are native to Central America. They are also popular with homeowners. You can start your own tree by rooting a seed in water. You can plant any time of year; plant them high, so the top of the large seed is well above the soil level. Choose a site with full sun and plenty of room above and below the ground, because this is a large tree. (Depending upon the species and variety, avocado trees can range from twenty to eighty feet tall.) Once established, it's drought tolerant, but it will produce more fruit with regular irrigation.

Avocados do not ripen on the tree. Wait until they are full-sized (for their variety) before you harvest them, and they'll ripen in about a week. The harvesting season can last from late spring through winter. Once the tree gets large, you may wish to invest in a long-handled avocado picker with a built-in basket. This device can also be used for other tree fruit. It's a good idea to pick your fruit before squirrels get them.

Laurel wilt disease can kill avocado trees. It is a fungal disease carried by a beetle that came to the United States in 2004 in pallet wood in Savannah, Georgia. The beetle and its deadly fungus can affect most members of the laurel family, including the red bay tree (*Persea borbonia*) and sassafras (*Sassafras albidum*), and it has been moving south. Ask your local extension service agent if it is a problem in your area or if there are cultivars resistant to this disease.

Bananas

Bananas (*Musa* spp.) are in their own family (Musaceae). They are a tender crop that's native to India and southeastern Asia. Even though they are called trees, there is no wood, only fiber holding them up. Once established, a banana plant will consist of a fibrous mat in the ground with several "trunks" that each bear a single large flower head that will develop into a stalk of fruit. When it's grown in North Florida, the trunks are killed back before the fruit can be harvested, so it's best to plant it further south.

Bananas need rich, damp soil, but not standing water, because without enough nutrients or water, the trunks might collapse under the weight of the fruit. Blooms develop ten to eighteen months after a trunk begins to grow. Fruit ripens about five months later. After the oldest bananas in the bunch begin to turn yellow, cut the entire bunch from the main stalk. Don't cut the trunk after the harvest, because the leaves will continue to produce energy for the plant.

Growing Vegetables Is Beneficial

Every pound of food that you grow, or buy from local growers, offsets up to two pounds of greenhouse gas emissions. We are so fortunate in Florida that we can have productive edible crops on a year-round basis. Grow more food for your family's health and for the health of our only planet.

Resources

Organic Methods for Vegetable Gardening in Florida, by Ginny Stibolt and Melissa Contreras. We cover everything from building soil to just-in-time harvesting.

The University of Florida's Institute of Food and Agricultural Sciences (IFAS) is our state agricultural extension service, with offices in each county. IFAS offers many services—both online and in person—including data sheets on crops, soil testing, plant identification, the Master Gardener program, and more; to find your local office, visit http://sfyl.ifas.ufl.edu/.

7

◌

Soil, Compost, and Mulch

Most of Florida has sandy and somewhat acidic soil, but in South Florida and some other areas, the limestone base makes that soil more alkaline, and in North Florida there are regions with clay soils similar to those in Georgia. As gardeners, we can improve any of these soils by adding compost and by mulching the surfaces. I covered some of this in the chapter on lawns, but here we'll dig a bit deeper. When we take care of the soil, it will take care of the plants!

Florida's Soils

Soil is *so* much more than just dirt. Soil found in native habitats is a complex ecosystem: a web of bacteria, fungi, nematodes, earthworms, ants, salamanders, toads, insect larvae, moles, and more all living in a substrate of minerals and humus. The minerals are a mixture of rocks, sand, silt, or clay. The humus or organic matter consists of fully or partially digested plant and animal parts. As humus is broken down into simple compounds, it provides a living for the decomposers and eventually yields nutrients for plants.

One gram of healthy, nonpoisoned soil (about one-fifth of a teaspoon, depending on moisture and soil type) could contain one hundred million bacteria, one million actinomycetes (a special type of bacteria that provide the signature "good-soil" smell), and one hundred thousand fungi—if strung together, the fungal filaments (hyphae) would measure about sixteen feet in length. This same gram of soil could also contain hundreds of nematodes (which are mostly beneficial) living on the damp surfaces of the soil particles, and maybe a few insect eggs or larvae and some earthworm cocoons. The exact proportions of each of these organisms will depend on soil conditions such as acidity, moisture, aeration, amount of humus, and the local plant community.

Soil acidity is measured on the pH (potential of hydrogen) scale, with a pH of 1 being most acidic and a pH of 14 being most alkaline. Most plants grow well in a slightly acidic soil—a pH between 6 and 7, but some plants are adapted to highly acidic soils and other plants thrive in alkaline soils. Chemical conditions including acidity will influence the balance of local organism populations. Fungi are more plentiful in acidic soils, while actinomycetes and other bacteria prefer more alkaline conditions. You cannot readily change the nature of your soil's acidity for the long run, so it's best to live with the soil chemistry you have and to find native plants that occur naturally in such soils.

Soil texture is determined by its relative portions of sand, silt, and clay particles. These proportions are also not easy to change. Although it seems logical, you should not add sand to a clay soil, because you are likely to end up with a cement-like material. You can improve soil structure, whether it is sandy or clayey, by adding compost. In a native or mostly native landscape, it's best to use compost made from local materials and with no added manures.

Note: Don't use peat moss to amend your soil. There is no sustainable way to harvest peat. It takes hundreds of years to form under special anaerobic conditions, and efforts to restore mined peat fields result in more CO_2 being released than sequestered. So while peat moss adds humus and absorbs moisture, it is extremely acidic and provides virtually no nutrients. A viable substitute is coconut coir, a by-product of the coconut industry. Absorbent and neutral in its acidity, coir also provides nutrients. Coir is used to make products that have traditionally been made from peat, such as mats used to line hanging baskets and little pots to start seeds. The one big drawback of coir is its transportation footprint, because most of it is produced in Indonesia.

You can get some idea of what your native soil might have been like before development by consulting the detailed soil maps available online and at your local extension office, and also, as previously discussed, by knowing what your native plant community was before development (which also provides a good guideline for what to plant). In many Florida neighborhoods, non-native soil was imported as part of the development process, especially in low-lying areas. If that's the case, then there may not be any truly native soil present in your landscape. No matter what the soil is, you can improve it to host a diverse native plant community or a bountiful vegetable garden in your yard.

HYDROPHOBIC SOIL

Hydrophobic is defined as "afraid of water." When the term is used to describe soil, its meaning is modified to "repels water." This is important to us as gardeners, because if water is not being absorbed into the soil, it is not available to the roots of our plants.

This is particularly serious for newly germinated seedlings, which must have even moisture supplied by the soil during their initial growth period. A scarcity of water can kill newly sprouted seeds with their tiny root systems. Also, newly planted trees, shrubs, or herbaceous specimens are already stressed and in extreme need of water to

When water is applied to very dry soil, it may only wet the top one-eighth of an inch of soil. While the surface of the soil looks wet and additional water runs off, the underlying hydrophobic soil remains dry.

rehydrate their leaves, so that photosynthesis can take place to provide as much energy as possible during their transition into new locations.

To understand what is happening here, let's back up a bit to look at water's chemistry. Water is made up of two hydrogen atoms and one oxygen atom, giving it the familiar chemical formula of H_2O. The hydrogen atoms attach themselves to one side of the oxygen, covering about one-third of a sphere, so that the molecules look very much like a Mickey Mouse head. The side of the molecule with the hydrogen atoms has a slight positive charge, and the oxygen side is slightly negative. Water molecules act like little magnets; they are attracted to each other and form weak bonds called hydrogen bonds. You notice this self-attraction (cohesion) when water beads up into droplets. And this is important for gardeners to know when we are dealing with both plants and soil.

It's best to use untreated water from lakes, wells, or rain barrels for irrigating your plants, both in your gardens and in containers. The reason for this is that tap water is treated with purifiers to kill bacteria, fungi, and viruses so that it's safe for us to drink. But those purifiers also kill the soil microbes. Healthy soil and good, rich compost are dependent on an ecosystem consisting of millions of microbes. If all you have is tap water, it's best to let it sit for a day or two to give the volatile chemicals a chance to evaporate. (More on rain barrels in chapter 8.)

Since water clings to itself, if soil is moist, there will not be a problem with water soaking in, because all the water molecules that are already clinging to the particles of soil will bond with the incoming water. But if the soil has dried out so much that very little water is clinging to soil particles, then the newly applied water will not readily soak in—it may only wet the soil's surface, and additional water will not soak in, but run off. Or in a container, the water may seep out around the edges of the pot without wetting the soil.

In general, more organic material in the soil will reduce hydrophobic tendencies, because organic materials absorb and hold more water. As discussed previously, when I build my wide row beds for my edibles, I create a slight swale in the planting surfaces so water will sit on the soil and eventually soak in. If I'm hand irrigating a new crop, I'll irrigate each row, let it sit until it soaks in, and then irrigate again, until I've added enough water so the soil is damp to at least an inch below the soil surface. It's called the knuckle test: the soil should be damp to at least the first joint on your index finger.

Undisturbed soil will hold a lot more moisture than soil that has been disturbed from plowing, seasonal planting, or pulling weeds. This is important to know for your general landscaping areas. Minimize disturbance when pulling weeds; in the case of annual weeds, you may be able to just cut them off at the base to weaken them. Undisturbed soil is also better for the climate, because disturbed soil releases more carbon into the atmosphere.

THE RHIZOSPHERE

The rhizosphere is the area around the roots of a plant where the plant and the soil inhabitants interface, and it begins to form as soon as a seed germinates. In healthy soil, the microbial community is activated as the seed secretes its chemical signals into the soil. Genetic information is exchanged; the various microbial players assume their positions on the tissues of the plant. Sometimes the microbes are nitrogen-fixing bacteria such as rhizobia, which form root nodules on legumes and help them to grow well in poor soil. But more often it is a mycorrhizal fungus that forms a symbiotic relationship with the roots. These collective relationships are called mycorrhizae.

Mycorrhizae work because the fungi colonize the root system of a host plant, expanding its water and nutrient absorption capabilities, while the plant provides the fungus with carbohydrates formed from photosynthesis. In addition, mycorrhizae sometimes offer the host plant increased protection against certain pathogens.

Fungi emit chemicals into the soil in order to break down the organic materials in the soil and absorb their nutrients directly from the soil. Plants often have difficulty obtaining and absorbing major nutrients such as nitrogen and phosphorus, so fungi greatly increase the surface area that is open to nutrient and water absorption. The mycorrhizal relationship provides access to these essential compounds and elements for the plants. In return, the plant supplies the fungus with sugars. Approximately 90 percent of all vascular land plants live in some association with mycorrhizal fungi. (More on other types of fungi below.)

In addition, these mycorrhizae allow trees and other plants to communicate with each other and even trade nutrients, so that the whole plant community works cooperatively. Given all the complexity of a healthy soil ecosystem, just think what happens when a lawn service applies a general fungicide to your landscape. This intricate dance of fungi and plant roots, which is so important to the health of plants, is halted. The health of the plants will be negatively impacted: they may not die right away, but their growth and vigor will certainly decline.

Compost

You can encourage soil recovery by adding compost. Keep in mind that compost is not used in the same manner as an artificial fertilizer. Instead, it is usually applied more generously and serves a different role than synthetic fertilizers.

Adding compost to your soil has many benefits:

* it adds humus, which improves soil texture;
* it increases water retention;
* it provides some nutrients; and
* it increases the populations of soil microbes, which is its most important function.

To keep soil disturbance to a minimum, do not dig it in when applying to the general landscape. The compost will be absorbed into the soil as its soil organisms work. As described in the chapter on lawns, after the poisons are stopped, a thin layer of compost speeds up the recovery of the underlying soil ecosystem, but this should only happen in early spring when the grass is actively growing and when it's still the dry season when no rain is forecasted, because you don't want it to wash away. And as described in the chapter on trees and shrubs, you can apply compost as a topdressing to the soil around and outside of the planting holes of selected plants that you wish to encourage. For wildflower meadows and most natural or native landscapes, you'd probably not use much compost, because the native wildflowers and bunching grasses are adapted to low-nutrient soil and because the enriched soil would tend to attract weeds.

As mentioned above, for native landscapes or freedom lawns, do not use manures in your compost, because their high nutrient levels may push the plants into unnatural growth spurts and encourage weeds that would otherwise not grow in that environment. Your goal here is to encourage a more resilient landscape with a natural growth cycle.

In your vegetable beds and for other edible crops, however, herbivore manures (cow, horse, rabbit, and chicken) are often recommended to build soil there, because your goal is to grow crops quickly and to promote a bountiful harvest. Also, soil disturbance is mostly unavoidable as you cycle through crops for each season.

BUILDING COMPOST

When we moved to Florida in 2004, I found an out-of-the-way spot on our lot for a compost pile and started out using the most informal method for composting: when I had leaves, weeds, or clippings, I piled them on top. I didn't turn the pile or pay attention to whether the materials were "brown" or "green." ("Brown" materials are carbon-rich items such as dried leaves, straw, shredded paper, and wood chips. "Green" materials are nitrogen-rich and moist; they include grass clippings, weeds, coffee grounds, and kitchen scraps.) I knew composting was happening, because the pile stayed the same size for more than a year and a half of heavy gardening—approximately three feet in all directions.

When we decided to establish a vegetable garden in the bed at the back of the house, we knew that the very sandy soil there needed enrichment, so it was time to harvest the compost. I set aside the top layer of recently deposited and uncomposted waste and dug into the heart of the compost pile. The beautiful, crumbly compost smells like the forest floor because of the actinomycetes: members of a group of bacteria that act like fungi and play a big part in the rotting process that turns plant materials into compost.

Finished compost doesn't look like any of the materials used to build the pile.

General Composting Guidelines

There's a lot of good information about composting techniques; here is what has worked for us in Florida:

* Do add gardening waste (weeds and trimmings), but not diseased plants or noxious weeds.
* Use equal amounts of green and brown materials.
* Do add kitchen scraps, but not meat, oils, or dairy.
* Keep compost moist, but not wet.
* No manures should be included for general landscape use. But for edible beds, you may add manure from horses, cows, chickens, or rabbits; don't use dog, cat, or human feces (although human urine is okay).
* Don't add twigs larger than the width of your finger: they take too long to decompose.
* The composting materials need to have enough mass for the microbes' activity to raise the temperature. To allow air into the pile, the rule of thumb is that the pile needs to be at least three feet in any direction, but not greater than five feet in height or width, but it can be as long as needed. Make sure the compost pile is at least two feet from any building.

The more often you turn the pile, the faster it will become fully composted. ("Turning" is rearranging the pile so the materials that were on top are on the bottom, and the materials on the outside are on the inside.) You can use a bin or not. A bin may be neater and easier to turn, but a bin will limit the amount of compost.

Composting is actually a form of fermentation, as the microbes break down the sugars in the plant and animal materials. When this happens, it heats up and you can see steam rising from the pile. For the

The fermentation of plant materials begins quickly. This load of wood chips from a local tree cutter began to steam the morning after delivery. A similar reaction happens in a well-built compost pile with equal amounts of green and brown materials.

fastest compost formation, as soon as it stops heating up, turn it, and it will heat up again. When it no longer heats up, it's done.

My Composting Strategy

As I started growing more vegetables, I realized that I needed a more efficient compost production scheme than my informal throw-everything-on-the-pile method. I could spend all my time adjusting the compost pile, if I followed all the advice. I could take its temperature to gauge its activity, turn it as soon as the heat dissipates, buy special composting worms, test the acidity, and add organic fertilizer or lime to adjust for nutrient levels and acidity. Whew! Too much work.

I designed my own simplified plan, because I'd rather spend my time actually gardening instead of tending to the compost. I have two separate compost piles: one that's carefully built over a week or two, which I keep moist during dry weather, and the other a wait-pile for new deposits that will be incorporated into the next carefully built pile. This two-pile method works well for me, but you may have different needs and resources in your yard.

First, the carefully built pile generates finished compost fairly quickly—in two or three months. I build a new, 3' × 3' × 5' pile in alternating layers: a) brown materials: dead leaves, shredded paper, partially decomposed wood chips, and other dead plant materials from the wait-pile such as pulled St. Augustine grasses; b) green materials: kitchen scraps, freshly pulled weeds, green clippings, water hyacinth (*Eichhornia crassipes*) if available from the lake, pond muck, and coffee grounds; c) thin layers of soil or finished compost to add microbes. After each set of layers, I irrigate with one watering can of rain-barrel water and stick a garden fork into all areas of the top of the pile and rock the fork back and forth. This creates passages between the layers and consolidates and spreads out the materials. This way, the pile keeps its form and remains flat on the top. It usually takes a week or two to build a pile, so when I stop for the day, I cover that last layer with a layer of pine needles. Later, I scrape them off before continuing the layering during the next session. When the pile is big enough, I cover the whole pile with a good, thick layer of pine needles. The purpose for the layering is to manage the 50:50 ratio of brown to green materials so that it will heat up. I may or may not turn the pile depending upon my need for more compost. Once the turning process begins, the layers will be obliterated, but that's okay. If the compost smells of ammonia or if it has a sour smell, turn the pile and layer in brown materials to dry it out. Dry leaves are a good choice for this purpose. The pile will reduce in size as the microbes do their work.

(Note: I used to pull invasive water hyacinths from the lake at the back of our lot. This plant contains lots of good nutrients that produce richer compost, but in the last five years or so, the lake has been treated, so this has not been readily available.)

Then there's the wait-pile. This pile is passive: I add garden waste as I generate it. This is what I did before, and it works fine, but it's slow. I have used the wait-piles not only for building new balanced piles but also for composting-in-place when preparing my edible beds.

Composting in Place

In addition to building the compost piles, I also compost in place in both new and established vegetable beds. You could also modify this to build soil for container gardens.

There are two ways that I compost in place: trench composting, mainly with kitchen scraps, and layering in the beds to create new soil or to refresh old soil after several seasons of crops.

TRENCH COMPOSTING

Burying kitchen scraps in the vegetable beds or in the compost pile is an ongoing process, because there are always peels, cores, stems, and more leftovers from cooking. No meat scraps or other animal products should be included. I collect kitchen scraps in a metal bucket with a vented top with filters to keep the odor down. It sits on the kitchen counter. When it's been a few days or if it's full, then I dump it somewhere in the garden, or if I don't have a spot in the beds, I bury it in the top of the compost pile. You are not limited to kitchen scraps; you could also use the remnants of your crops (as long as they are not diseased), grass clippings, shredded paper waste, or other green compost materials.

Burying kitchen scraps into the vegetable beds is one form of composting-in-place and is a sustainable use for your organic wastes. Our house was equipped with a garbage disposal, but we've never used it.

If I'm working on a bed, it could be a total bed composting project between crop seasons, or it could be in the bottom of a swale or between the wide rows while the plants are small. You don't want to disturb the roots after the crops have matured—the goal is to have these scraps be totally composted by the time the crop roots hit the bottom of the swale or into the bottom of the trench.

For trench composting in the beds, I first remove the mulch, then dig the trench another four or five inches deeper, lay in a three-inch layer of kitchen scraps, cover it with one or two inches of soil, and then replace the mulch. For my situation, I use pine needles as mulch in the vegetable gardens, whether I'm working on a total bed project or a between-the-rows project. After completing one load, I'll dig the hole in preparation for the next batch. This way I can keep track of where I want to place the next load.

LAYERED COMPOSTING

When I'm building new beds and need new soil, I first remove all the plant materials from the area, especially deep-rooted weeds. Then I begin the layers with a thick layer of dead leaves raked from the yard, which will hold the moisture and will decompose into rich soil. Oak leaves are a good choice because they'll last a bit longer. I then add alternating layers of green and brown materials as if I were building a compost pile until the soil level is more than a foot above grade. If I have a good supply of unfinished compost or materials from the wait-pile, I will include that into the layering. Then I cover the new bed with a thick layer of pine needles to keep it moist and to keep the worms in place. In a month or so, it should be ready to form into wide rows. If I have finished compost, at that time, I'll add it into the top level of the wide rows to provide a finer substrate for the seeds or plants.

If I'm refurbishing an existing bed, I'll shovel out the top six inches of soil and hold it in the cart or wheelbarrow. Then I'll add a three-inch layer of green materials including kitchen scraps, and if they're available, I include marigold stems; then I add half of the soil back and a layer of finished or unfinished compost, and finally I replace the rest of the soil on top. I'll cover it with pine needles and keep it damp for a week or more before creating wide rows or swales.

I was preparing this square bed next to the garage for okra. Since okra is susceptible to root-knot nematodes, the majority of that green layer was marigold stems.
The soil in the cart was used to cover the green materials. To make the task more
manageable, I do this for half the bed and then do the second half later. After a
week or so, I created swales for the okra and planted the seeds. The crop grew so
tall that year that Dean and I needed a stepladder to harvest them. When I pulled
the plants at the end of the season, there was no root damage from nematodes.

Every Gardener Needs to Compost

Every gardener needs to compost for better soil: whether you have
sandy soil, like we do, or clay soil, compost is the answer. Plus, recycling
our yard waste into compost is the right thing to do: our taxes are
paying for bigger and bigger landfills to accommodate more and more
waste. Composting not only is good for gardens, but also allows all of
us to live more gently.

Mulch

Mulch is a material used to cover bare soil. Mulch can be organic,
such as wood chips, shredded wood, bark chunks, and pine needles, or

inorganic, such as rocks or gravel. In general, gardeners want to cover the soil to hold in moisture, reduce weeds, and moderate temperature changes. Another reason for using mulch is to reduce ongoing landscape maintenance. But there are some cases where mulch is not beneficial, such as around citrus shrubs and in developing meadows or wildflower gardens, because mulches reduce reseeding of most native flowers and grasses.

Here in Florida, with our year-round gardening, we have several items to consider when choosing mulch, and there are some commonly sold mulching products that are unsustainable or simply do not work. In addition, there are some big mulching mistakes commonly made in "professionally" maintained Florida landscapes that set a bad example for novice gardeners and for people new to the state. I admit that I've made some questionable mulching choices, but I'm relating them here so you can avoid some of these mulching mistakes.

Weed Barrier Cloth

While not a mulch, we need to discuss weed barrier cloth or geotextile here, since it's often used with mulches. When we bought our house, the former owners gave us a quick tour of the property. As we walked along the bed between the sidewalk and the front porch, the wife said, "Now *you* get to weed this bed." They had planted a series of dwarf yaupon holly (*Ilex vomitoria* var. 'Nana') shrubs as foundation plants and bunches of variegated lilyturf (*Liriope muscari*) near the sidewalk. They'd covered the soil with reddish volcano gravel. (More on using rocks as mulch below.) She was right: it was a weed haven.

The next spring, Dean and I decided that we would "fix" this bed for good. I pulled out the weeds and the lilyturf and harvested the gravel to use elsewhere. We added some pond muck to the bed since the soil level seemed too low. We bought thirty-year, nonwoven weed barrier cloth and many plastic bags of cypress mulch. We were confident that we'd "handled" the problem of the front bed. Ha!

We'd made several beginner mistakes in this project. Yes, it looked good for several months, but this is Florida, and weeds came back with a vengeance, both on top of that mulch and from under the weed

Our heavy-handed attempt to "fix" the weediness of the front bed included weed barrier cloth and many bags of cypress mulch. In this photo, we've removed the gravel and added the fill to the front of the bed, and it was waiting for the weed barrier cloth. The foundation plants included a gardenia (*Gardenia* sp.), several dwarf yaupon hollies (*Ilex vomitoria* 'Nana'), and a sago palm (*Cycas revoluta*). Sagos are not palms at all, but are cycads from Japan.

barrier cloth. The roots of both the weeds and the shrubs grew right through the cloth, and only a few years later, we ripped it all out—such a huge waste of time, effort, and money, not to mention its carbon footprint in both manufacture and space in our landfills. Also, today, I'd never buy cypress mulch, because it's not a sustainable product. (See page 125 for more on this mulch.)

Those cute yaupon hollies grew, and pretty soon, as discussed previously, they had grown out to the sidewalk and back to the porch. Dean bought a battery-powered hedge trimmer to keep them away from the porch and sidewalk and maintain their height at about four and a half feet. The weeds were no longer much of a problem, because these shrubs were so large and thick. I did transplant some fogfruit (*Phyla nodiflora*) from the lawn to the edge of the bed. Now, the gardenia is gone and so is the sago, and as I discussed previously, the yaupon hollies had died back, and Dean trimmed them back to approximately the size they were when we moved in. So now I had my weed-magnet bed again, but this time, I was prepared with a better plan. I filled the areas with more fogfruit and bunches of wildflowers either transplanted from other areas in the yard or planted by seed. It's a bit unruly, but there's not much room left for the weeds; when they do sneak in, I pull them, so gradually I've encouraged the plants I want and pulled the ones I considered to be weeds. The basic strategy here has been to crowd out the weeds with wildflowers.

Note: While weed barrier cloth or landscape fabric is basically ineffective in preventing weeds in Florida landscapes when covered by rocks or mulch, there are some places where it is useful in keeping soil from entering or escaping. We have used it to line dry wells large and small to keep soil from filling spaces between gravel, which keeps those gaps open to retain more water. Landscape fabric can also be used as a liner behind retaining walls and other structures to allow water to escape but not the soil.

Newspaper or Cardboard

These paper products are a much better option than weed barrier cloth. As discussed in the chapter on lawns, layers of newspaper or cardboard will kill grass and shallow-rooted weeds, and if you add a thick layer of wood-based mulch, shredded dry leaves, or both on top of it, that might be somewhat more effective than mulch alone. Until the paper rots, it does inhibit soil critters from free access to the mulch and sometimes, before the paper layer rots, there may be a buildup mold. Be sure to slice through the paper when you install plants, but this is not necessary if you've sowed seeds.

Rocks

In more arid landscapes, rocks and gravel can work very well as a mulch and will need almost no upkeep. Sometimes the rocks are so artfully arranged with contrasting colors and shapes that they look like beautiful mosaics. In Florida, however, with our fifty inches of rain,

In 2008, three years after installation and just after being cleaned out, the prickly pear rock-scape looks good. This was close to my vision and those cactus flowers really do attract the pollinators.

continual leaf drop, rampant weeds, and red imported fire ants, the rocks fill up with soil. With soil comes the weeds. In addition, rocks retain the heat better than soil, and that creates a new hot microclimate for that area. And gravel can be lofted by high winds and thrown by mowers. Once gravel is placed in an area without landscape fabric separating it from the soil, it will work its way into the soil and you'll never be rid of it.

My rock-scaping project started simply enough in 2005 when someone gave me a few pads of prickly pear cactus (*Opuntia stricta*), a Florida native. I had no clear idea what I was going to do with them, but you know how it is. It seemed like a good idea at the time, so I rooted them in a couple of pots. My new rock-scape became part of the front bed project when we'd pulled out all of that lava gravel. There were several larger volcanic rocks as well. Dean capped a sprinkler

I've had to clear out this rock-scape every couple of years to remove the soil and leaves from the gravel. I did have a layer of weed barrier cloth here to keep the gravel separate from the soil. This photo is from 2018; a couple of years prior, I'd added a Spanish bayonet (*Yucca aloifolia*) to the hill. The cacti had aged and their base pads had turned gray, so I cut back the old ones and started rooting new pads from the tops of the plants. They're in the shadows in this photo, but they looked okay. Two years later, however, I gave up, pulled the prickly pears, removed the weed barrier cloth, and replaced the gravel with woodchip mulch.

head at the intersection of the driveway and the front sidewalk, and we built up a mound so the cacti would have an appropriate hot and dry habitat.

Is rock-scaping sustainable in Florida? In most cases, no! It's a lot of work, and as far as my back is concerned, it is not sustainable from a maintenance perspective. But when it was cleaned up, I liked it and the pollinators really liked the cactus flowers, but after years of trying to keep even this small rock-scape neat, we took it all out and saved the volcanic gravel for another dry well or for some other project.

Rubber Mulch

While recycling old tires by shredding them and using them as mulch seems like a good, sustainable idea, it's not. As it degrades, the rubber will release toxins that kill soil microbes and other soil organisms. Plus, like rocks, it will never become part of the soil and will be impossible to remove once it works its way into the soil. Don't use it.

Wood Mulches

There are a number of different wood-based products that are used as mulch. Here are some examples:

* **Shredded cypress:** while it's a satisfactory mulch, whole cypress forests have been torn down to supply our mulching needs. At this point, it's not a sustainable product.
* **Shredded melaleuca** is an effective mulch that's mostly available in South Florida. Melaleuca trees (*Melaleuca quinquenervia*), also known as punk trees or paperbark tea trees, are native to Australia and are on the Category I list of invasives in Central and South Florida. Using this mulch helps finance its removal, especially from the Everglades.
* **Pine bark** is chunkier than other wood-based mulches and tends to last somewhat longer in the landscape. Don't use it in rain gardens or other areas where standing or running water is likely, because it will float away.
* **Arborist wood chips** are the most sustainable, since they're not packaged or shipped. They are often available locally and generally at no charge. The tree trimmers would rather dump their loads in the neighborhood where they are working to avoid the drive to the landfill and the dumping fee. This is my favorite for paths and around the bases of newly planted trees, but not in the raised beds of my vegetable gardens.

When I hear tree cutters in the neighborhood, I ride my bike toward the noise and ask for their load. We've gone through more than twenty loads of chips on our property over the years and only once was my request been refused. After the dump, I invite the neighbors to use the chips in their landscapes as well. We have the space off to the side of the front meadow area and the pile becomes a neighborhood asset.

Wood-based mulches are great for four reasons:

* They help hold in the moisture.
* They moderate temperature fluctuations.
* They reduce the germination of weed seeds, both physically, by smothering them, and chemically, when freshly applied, because the decomposers deplete the nitrogen supply at the soil surface.

* They eventually become part of the soil and enrich the whole area. The resulting rich soil stimulates the roots to spread outward for healthier and more wind-tolerant trees. This type of mulching is also called sheet composting.

The ideal thickness of the mulch cover varies depending on where it's used. For a path, use five or six inches, which may last for two years or so before needing more chips. For killing an existing patch of vegetation, use eight or nine inches. Some people lay down cardboard or paper first. This method only works for "normal" weeds; those with deep roots or persistent rhizomes will grow right through the mulch and the cardboard. For mulching between existing plantings, such as groupings of trees and shrubs, use three or four inches when the plantings are fresh, but reduce the thickness over the years until the grove's own leaf fall provides enough volume.

Wood chips should not be piled against tree trunks or shrub stems. It's not uncommon to see "professionally" maintained landscapes with "volcano" mulching around tree trunks. This is bad for the trees in several ways. Most trees live longer if their root flares are above the soil line. The moisture in the mulch could cause fungal infestations on and under the bark, or it could stimulate the tree to form adventitious roots above the soil line, which could stress the tree during droughts when that pile of mulch will become extremely dry. The mulch can also form a crust and shed water away from the tree. Finally, mounds of mulch could house rodents that might chew into the tree. Mulching trees, especially newly planted trees, is a good idea—but no mulch should touch the trunk.

WHY NOT WOOD CHIPS IN THE VEGETABLE BEDS?

I don't use arborists' wood chips in our edible beds. There are two main reasons for this:

* Wood chips deplete nutrients as they come in contact with the soil, because the microbes become much more active. For path mulches, this is an advantage for keeping down weeds, but we work so hard to increase the nutrient level in our edible gardens,

why compromise it in any way? Eventually, the chips decompose and add nutrients and humus to the soil, but not at first.

✳ Wood chips are impossible to remove completely from the soil. For other uses, like paths and more stable gardens, that's not a problem, but it doesn't work well with all the activity of changing crops at the end of each season.

Avoid Mulch-Only Landscapes

All too often I've seen lawns replaced with vast areas of mulch instead of dense plantings of natives or other sustainable plants. This seems to be more prevalent in commercial landscapes. It is not maintenance-free—mostly mulch landscapes are messy weed magnets and need regular care to stay reasonably good-looking. Seeds will land and take root on top of the mulch, and deep-rooted weeds will come up from the bottom—yes, even through weed barrier cloth, newspapers, or cardboard.

Mulch is a good idea for most landscapes where your planting design accounts for the eventual mature sizes of trees and shrubs. It keeps down weeds, it keeps in moisture, it reduces temperature fluctuations, and it eventually enriches the soil. But that doesn't mean that you need to lay down only mulch while you wait for your trees to grow.

A better idea is to plant bunching grasses and meadow wildflowers around your newly planted trees and shrubs and maintain it as a pollinator garden or meadow until the trees begin to cast significant shade. While you're waiting, it may be a good idea to mark or stake your trees and shrubs, so they are not hacked off by mistake during the annual cut of the meadow. When the trees start providing significant shade, it will be time to start modifying the area with shade-tolerant plants. Move the long-lived, sun-loving meadow plants out to the edges of your grove or to a new meadow area. The idea here is not to have a broad expanse of mulch while you're waiting for landscape plants to mature, but to establish a working ecosystem that will help turn that mulch into soil and reduce the problems with weeds.

Wood Mulches and Fungi

When you lay mulch in a path or in a garden, the microbes, including fungi, get to work. We don't normally notice the fungi until they produce their fruiting bodies, and here in Florida they can be quite diverse. In the vast majority of cases, there is nothing to worry about. Your plants will be fine.

Before we continue our discussion, let's cover some fungus fundamentals. When I took biology, there were two kingdoms of living things, the plants and the animals. Fungi were grouped with the plants, but now there are five kingdoms, and fungi have their own kingdom. Most soil fungi start as a spore and grow a long, threadlike white or clear hollow tube called a hypha, with or without dividing walls called septae. A mass or web of hyphae is called a mycelium. Hence the study of fungi is called mycology.

A lovely, fungal forest sprang from wood chips in a newly established pollinator garden in the front bed where the sago used to be.

Stinkhorn fungi! The first two years in our house when there was still some red-dyed cypress mulch, I'd find these six- or seven-inch-tall Ravenel's stinkhorns (*Phallus ravenelii*). They sprout up overnight from an egg-like sack; the spores are in the brown slime, which has the odor of feces. They wither by the end of the day. I also used to find octopus stinkhorns (*Clathrus columnatus*), which look like an orange cage with brown slime that smells of carrion; their odor is much stronger than Ravenel's stinkhorn. Once that red mulch was gone and I'd switched to arborist wood chips, I rarely see (or smell) these surprising fungi.

Fungi don't ingest their food like animals do, and they don't manufacture their own food the way plants do. Instead, fungi secrete digestive enzymes to break down the soil particles or other material to be digested, which releases the nutrients that they then can absorb. Basically, by releasing these enzymes, the fungi turn the soil around them into an external stomach. Plants in the area can also absorb those fungi-released nutrients.

As part of their life cycle, fungi produce spores. The sexual phase begins when hyphae from two different fungal organisms meet and fuse. The resulting fungal fruiting body could be a mushroom, a beautiful turkey tail, or an obnoxious stinkhorn. The fruiting body produces spores and is also the part of a fungus that allows us to identify it without a microscope. Slime molds, by the way, have a similar life cycle, but they are not fungi. There are a number of them that we might see in Florida. Most have a finer texture than fungal fruiting bodies. A typical example is dog vomit slime mold (*Fuligo septica*), which is well named for its look. Like fungi, slime molds are not generally harmful and will just disappear after a few days.

Most fungi are saprophytes, feeding on dead or decaying material, but some fungi are parasitic, feeding on living organisms. Some are symbiotic—the fungi live in a mutually beneficial relationship with another organism, as some do with plant roots, which we discussed above, or partnered with algae and bacteria to form lichens.

Fallen Leaves

Of course, fallen leaves are the most natural mulch. The sustainable gardening advice on raking leaves from your lawn is to leave the leaves so that various pollinators that hide among the leaf litter can complete their life cycles. On the other hand, a thick covering of leaves can kill the lawn. But if you have bunches of trees like we do, or if you have neighbors who diligently rake their leaves, you may have leaves available for use in the landscape. You may use them wherever you use wood-based mulch, but with two major problems: First, unless you've shredded them, they'll blow away when they dry out; second, the leaves will mat together if they get wet. Leaves can be used for paths where they'll be walked on often enough to keep them in place. If they are used with other mulching material, the leaves can increase the opacity of the mulch, to better shade out and smother grasses and the like. As previously described, I use leaves in building compost.

Pine Needles

Pine needles can be used as mulch wherever you'd use a wood-based mulch. They do not decompose as quickly as leaves or wood and they don't form a crust, so they are useful as a general mulch. But I use most of my pine needles in the vegetable beds. Pine needle mulch is good for several reasons:

* It does a good job at limiting weeds.
* It doesn't form a crust, so even a light rain filters to the soil and doesn't roll away.
* It is easy to handle and remove, which is important when used in vegetable beds when it's time for a crop change.
* It lasts for two years or more.
* It does not significantly acidify the soil below, since the decomposition is so slow.
* It is free, if there are pine trees in your neighborhood. I rake them from the street, and I have a neighbor with many more pines in his yard than ours who delivers his excess pine needles to my pile.

I use a thick layer of pine needles around the outsides of the raised beds and in the trenches between the wide-row planting areas. I use a very light layer of pine needles over the planting area where I've planted seeds. For larger-seeded or sturdier crops like squash, onions, or garlic, I mulch the planting surface with about an inch of pine needles—the crops will grow right through it.

I use a thick layer of pine needles on the beds after the soil has been prepared to reduce the weeds and keep in the moisture. When I'm ready to plant, I use a leaf rake to clear the pine needles away. After the crop has been harvested, I rake the pine needles across the lawn to allow the soil to fall away. Then they are ready to reuse for the next crop.

Straw

Straw and hay bales are usually available at farm supply stores. You want straw, not hay, for mulching because the straw does not include the seeds. It's usually harvested from grain crops where all the seeds have been harvested, so you only end up with the stems. Hay includes seeds, which is fine as bedding for horses and such, but you don't want those seeds introduced into your gardens.

Pine needles are the ideal mulch in vegetable gardens. They are easy to control, they don't form a crust, and they last a few years. Here, pine needles are neatly lined up in between a newly sprouted garlic crop.

Straw is a traditional mulch for vegetable gardens, and if you don't have access to pine needles, straw can be used in similar ways, but it doesn't last as long. Straw is also used as a light mulch after general broadcast seeding for meadows and such. Disadvantages to using straw in areas other than vegetable gardens are that it's so lightweight that it blows away, and also, in my opinion, it never looks natural or blends in the way pine needles or wood chips do.

Straw bales can also be used as instant raised beds to expand your vegetable garden space without any soil preparation. They are especially useful in areas where there are soil problems or as a growing medium for potatoes, so you don't have to dig to retrieve the tubers at the end of the season.

Soil Is Important

We have to stop treating our soil like dirt! As gardeners, good soil is our most important asset. While here in Florida, we might not have the best soil to start with, there are so many ways to improve this important ecosystem beneath our feet. When we take care of our soil, it takes care of our plants.

8

Stormwater Management

According to the U.S. Environmental Protection Agency, nonpoint source pollution is the leading cause of water pollution in the country, and our human-altered landscapes play a large role in this problem. In urban and suburban areas, much of the land surface is covered by buildings, pavement, and compacted soils. These impermeable surfaces do not allow rain to soak into the ground, which greatly increases the volume and velocity of stormwater runoff.

Urban runoff carries several kinds of pollutants:

sediments from erosion;
oil, grease, and toxic chemicals from motor vehicles;
pesticides, nutrients, and organic matter from lawns and gardens;
viruses, bacteria, and nutrients from pet waste and failing septic
  systems; and
thermal pollution from impervious surfaces such as streets and
  rooftops.

These pollutants damage fish and wildlife populations, kill native vegetation, foul our drinking water, and make recreational areas unsafe and unpleasant. Yet in many Florida developments, the stormwater that falls on roofs and other impervious surfaces is piped directly out to the streets and into the storm drainage systems, which increases the already-huge runoff. But when we slow down or sequester more of the rainfall in our yards and in our communities, it improves the water quality and eases the load on storm drain systems. Forward-thinking towns and communities encourage rain-barrel use, and some communities even provide free or discounted rain barrels to their citizens. Just think how much the initial stormwater runoff would be reduced if just half of a town's citizens used a rain barrel or two!

Rainwater is not a waste product, but a valuable resource.

Reducing the runoff can be a two-pronged approach: First, collecting water from our roofs with rain barrels or cisterns, and second, sequestering stormwater in rain gardens, ponds, or dry wells. And because of our high volume of rainfall in the wet season, it's a good idea to plan for the overflow from rain barrels, rain gardens, and ponds into areas that can absorb the water, such as additional rain gardens or wooded areas.

Rain Barrels: "Savings for a Sunny Day!"

We brought one rain barrel with us from Maryland, but we added six more that Dean fashioned from fifty-five-gallon barrels that we picked up at a local bottling plant. We added three in 2004 and another three a few years later. That original barrel split, so now we have six. Over the years, we've come to depend on this supply of soft, untreated water for our inside plants, porch plants, and outside plants when general irrigation is not on or not adequate for certain plants, such as seedlings, transplants, and the vegetable gardens. In the winter when the lawn is dormant, we only turn on the irrigation system once a month or so, for only a few minutes, to exercise its parts. (The irrigation system pumps water from the lake.) The rain-barrel water is most important during this period for irrigating the vegetable gardens. During the wet season, the rain barrels are not as useful in the landscape, but they still absorb that initial flush of stormwater, which is useful in the reduction of water pollution.

As previously mentioned, the untreated water from rain barrels is much better for the soil because it does not kill the microbes that are so important for a functioning soil ecosystem. Tap water has been treated to kill bacteria, fungi, and mold so that our water is safe to drink, but killing microbes is the last thing you want to do to your soils. Rain-barrel water is not for human consumption because of bird droppings and other stuff that lands on your roof, but it's been proven safe for use in vegetable gardens, even from asphalt roofing. This is because the plants process nutrients for growth and filter out substances that are not useful to the plants.

Note that some roofing materials, such as cedar shakes, will have been treated with chemicals to reduce moss and algae growth and to preserve the wood. Rain barrels are not recommended for these roofs.

Water from rain barrels has a wide variety of uses:

* irrigating plants—both for inside plants and those in the landscape;
* wetting the compost piles;
* prerinsing veggies;
* prerinsing hands, feet, and maybe even dirty gardening socks;
* rinsing gardening gloves and muddy tools; and
* cleaning out pots and planters.

I'm sure you'll find many more uses for rain-barrel water! If you're like us, you'll wonder how you gardened without it.

Getting Started with Rain Barrels

The easiest, but more expensive method is to buy already configured rain barrels. Also, most agriculture extension offices offer rain-barrel workshops, where for a small fee, you learn how to build a rain barrel and end up with one to take home. You can also make a rain barrel or a rain-barrel system on your own with a few common tools, plumbing supplies from a hardware store, and a moderate amount of effort. Previous experience working with PVC plumbing fixtures is helpful. Dean built our rain barrels and learned how to build them from various resources on the internet.

First, you'll need the barrels. Fifty-five-gallon barrels are often available from bottling plants or food processing plants for free or for a small fee. You must make sure that the barrels have been used for food-grade products and not for poisons or petroleum products. When we picked up our barrels from a local bottling plant, we were surprised to see the explosive and caustic warnings on the syrup barrels, but the guy we talked to said that all soft drink syrup is explosive and caustic. I knew there was a reason why we don't drink that stuff. But these were still food-grade barrels.

Calculating the Rainfall Volume

So that you have an idea of how many rain barrels you'll need for your situation, here's how to calculate rainfall to gallons: If you collect rainwater from five hundred square feet of roof area (regardless of pitch), a one-inch rainfall will produce three hundred gallons of water. (I used to teach seventh- and eighth-grade math, so this would be one of those dreaded word problems.)

Here's the math: Gallons = 0.6 × (inches of rain) × (surface area in square feet). (The 0.6 is the conversion factor to translate inches of rainfall to gallons. Actually, 0.62333 is possible, but you won't collect every drop of rain. Some of it evaporates, or is blown off the roof, so 0.6 is a good estimate and easier on your brain.) If you receive one inch of rain, and a gutter/downspout collects rainwater from, say, one-fourth of a 2000-square-foot roof, or 2000 / 4 = 500 square feet, then:

> 0.6 × 1 inch × 500 square feet = 300 gallons of water from that downspout.

Our Rain Barrels

We have three separate rain-barrel systems—each with a different configuration. Two are open systems, where the overflow is directed elsewhere when the barrels fill up. The single barrel is a closed system, where the overflow backs up into the downspout from the barrel.

Mosquitoes

When I talk about rain barrels, often the first reaction is that there would be mosquitoes. Naturally, we've taken steps to prevent them:

* The collection points for the open systems are all covered with screening that prevents both mosquitoes and tree litter from entering the rain barrels.

These three tandem rain barrels have the downspout from the garage gutter emptying into the first barrel. Overflow hoses lead into the other two barrels, and a final overflow hose empties into my watering cans, which hold an extra five gallons, and then on to driveway pavement. From there, the water runs into an area where compost piles are located and to a swale in the landscape behind the shed. The first barrel has a plastic catch-basket with a screen to filter out the sticks and leaves from the roof and to reduce the risk of mosquito eggs in the standing water. This is an open system.

A single, closed-system barrel near our vegetable garden at the back of the house. The downspout has been interrupt-ed with an overflow diverter, which is designed so that when the barrel is full, the water backs up and drains into the downspout, which runs into a French drain that empties into a wooded area. The three-tiered cinder block tower provides enough height, so I can use a hose to irrigate the gardens.

* The industrial, food-grade barrels have a lip around the top. Dean drilled four holes in the lip of each barrel so that the water drains out. If he hadn't, an inch or so of water would sit on top of each barrel; if that doesn't evaporate or drain within three days, the mosquitoes would have time to lay their eggs and hatch.
* For the closed rain barrel, Dean punched out small weep holes in the bottom of the diverter, so the water that collects there when the barrel is full can slowly drain away.

We started with four rain barrels but found that these were not enough to serve our needs, especially in the dry season, which is our primary vegetable-growing season. Once you add a few rain barrels in your yard, you'll wonder how you gardened without that steady supply of

For this set of barrels, Dean built a four-foot-high deck to elevate the barrels, so the force of gravity provides some water pressure. These three barrels are tied together with a series of pipes through bottom fittings so that all the barrels fill up and drain together. Each of the barrels has its own overflow pipe, and these are all connected to another pipe, and then to a hose that drains away the excess water. This arrangement means that we can attach a hose to a single spigot to irrigate the beds, and that there is good pressure due to the height of the platform.

untreated water that is so much better for the soil, and therefore better for your plants. Also, soaking up all that stormwater will also improve the usability of your landscape—fewer soggy areas after Florida's hard rains.

Rain Gardens

Rain gardens and bioswales serve two main purposes:

1) to capture or slow down rainwater runoff in a low spot and to allow it to percolate through the soil and be absorbed by water-loving plants; and
2) to prevent soil erosion from fast-moving water. The runoff comes from gutter downspouts, French drain systems, or from impervious surfaces such as driveways, parking lots, and roads.

Of course, a rain garden with its water-tolerant plants will also look better than a drainage ditch. Rain gardens can be large or small and are designed to receive stormwater from roofs, driveways, or other impervious surfaces. Forward-thinking municipalities are including roadside rain gardens with curb cuts so that water collected on the roads drains into the swales.

When evaluating your own property, you may find there are some areas where rain gardens would be useful for sequestering stormwater, but there may be some areas where stormwater collected on impermeable surfaces is already handled. The runoff from our cement driveway did not require a rain garden because it is directed into a small wooded area, which is significantly lower than the driveway and where there are cinnamon ferns (*Osmundastrum cinnamomeum*), sweetgum trees (*Liquidambar styraciflua*), and wax myrtle shrubs (*Morella cerifera*), all of which tolerate and absorb the standing water.

When designing a rain-garden system, the aim is to have all the water soak into the soil, be absorbed by the rain-garden plants, or drain away in three days or less to keep the mosquitoes at bay. Plants in a rain garden need to tolerate both flooding and drought because here in Florida, we have that seven-month dry season. Keep in mind that larger plants with more leaf area will pull more water from the soil.

A mature tree can transpire more than three hundred gallons of water on a hot summer day, so if possible, for large rain gardens, include larger plants to more quickly absorb the water. For locations that can only host low-growing plants for visibility, the rain garden's surface area will need to be larger to absorb the same quantity of water.

Here are a few rain-garden plants recommended for Central and North Florida. Most of these plants will also work in South Florida, but in that region, there are some other tropical native plants that will also tolerate rain-garden conditions. (Note: These lists are for rain gardens that dry out in the dry season. If the soil stays wet, then there are several additional wetland plants that can be used.)

Herbaceous plants include black-eyed Susans (*Rudbeckia* spp.), blue-eyed grasses (*Sisyrinchium* spp.), climbing aster (*Symphyotrichum carolinianum*), dotted horsemint (*Monarda punctata*), eastern gamagrass or Fakahatchee grass (*Tripsacum dactyloides*), goldenrods (*Solidago* spp.), meadow garlic (*Allium canadense*), mistflower (*Conoclinium coelestinum*), rain lily (*Zephyranthes atamasca*), soft rush (*Juncus effusus*), and whitetop sedge (*Rhynchospora colorata*).

Woody plants include arrowwood (*Viburnum dentatum*), bald cypress (*Taxodium distichum*), beautyberry (*Callicarpa americana*), cabbage palm (*Sabal palmetto*), dahoon holly (*Ilex cassine*), elderberry (*Sambucus nigra*), inkberry (*Ilex glabra*), red maple (*Acer rubrum*), saltbush (*Baccharis halimifolia*), saw palmettos (*Serenoa repens*), sweetbay magnolia (*Magnolia virginiana*), and southern wax myrtle (*Morella cerifera*).

OUR RAIN GARDENS

At first, I built a few small rain gardens, starting with the easiest project, where a downspout at the corner of our front porch emptied directly into the lawn. I also created rain gardens at three outflows from French drains where I repaired the significant erosion, laid in some rocks to protect the soil from erosion, and built one or more wide swales where water can pool before it flows into the wooded drainage area or pond. These were out of view and in the shade, so my planting strategy was to just use ferns around the swales. Over the years these have worked well, and new plants have volunteered in these spaces.

There was not much erosion at the front porch downspout, but the lawn was really soggy after every downpour, and the plastic deflector was tipped toward the house, creating mosquito-attracting puddles after each rain. I removed almost two feet of lawn, reset the runoff tray, and built a small dry well by setting in some fake river stones (left over from building our house) over a deep bed of gravel. This is a partly sunny location, so I planted ferns: what I *thought* was native spleenwort (*Asplenium* sp.) and netted chain fern (*Woodwardia areolata*). I also planted rain lilies (*Zephyranthes atamasca*) and blue-eyed grass (*Sisyrinchium angustifolium*) alongside the rocks. I added some moss between the rocks to soften their appearance and make the installation look less new. I found out later that the fern I had believed to be native spleenwort was actually a lookalike called tuberous sword

A year after its installation, this downspout rain garden provides interest and slows down the outflows. But soon after this photo was taken, I removed the invasive tuberous sword ferns. No wonder they were doing so well.

The original rain garden is to the right in this photo. We dug out an area that bypassed the sprinkler head (with the green donut at the bottom center of the photo). We planned for the drainpipe to receive the rain garden overflow and to have enough slope away from the house for good drainage.

fern (*Nephrolepis cordifolia*), a Category I invasive plant in Florida. So I ripped out all the sword fern.

Note: If your house has a basement, locating a rain garden this close to the foundation would not be prudent. In this case, it is best to use a drainpipe to take water away from your foundation and install your rain garden so the draining water will not end up in your basement.

A few years later, I decided to expand the capacity of the downspout rain garden as part of my plan to replace that lawn with a mulched path and a fern garden. I didn't want to dig up the old rain garden, since it looked good and functioned fairly well, but there were some unmovable restrictions at this site in the form of a sprinkler head and three irrigation access points: covered wells with various switches for the underground irrigation pipes. Also, we didn't want the excess water to interfere with the pathway, so we'd need a blind drain to absorb the water and direct it under the path.

Designing the Drainage

Given the site restrictions and the need for a path, Dean and I arranged a ten-foot drainage pipe to lead from the end of the expanded rain garden opposite the downspout to a sandy area on the other side of the path near the pond. Then we dug the tear-drop-shaped rain-garden expansion area so the depths would work with the blind drain. The deeper area just past the original rain garden is about a foot deep and catches a significant amount of water, but when it fills up, the excess water flows into the blind drain. It has functioned well for years.

To fashion the blind drain, we dug a hole that is about a fourteen-inch cube, lined it with a four-foot square of landscape fabric, laid the fabric edges out on the sides of the hole, and filled it with a wheelbarrow load of clean lava rocks (the ones left by the previous owner). We wrapped the cloth around the rocks like a package, so the

Detail of the blind drain at the far end of the expanded rain garden, with cloth-covered gravel in the dry well and the abutting drainage pipe.

soil will not compromise their ability to collect water. I cut up a pair of old pantyhose, and a leg covers each end of the drainage pipe to keep the dirt out. We created a similar rock-filled hole at the far end of the pipe, making sure that that end of the pipe was lower in elevation to ensure good drainage away from the house and toward the pond. At each end, the pipe butts up against the cloth at a height that is even with the tops of the holes. At the front end, this means that the water won't flow into the pipe until all the spaces between the rocks are filled to the top. At the far end, water from the pipe dumps into the top of another rock-filled hole.

After we had the drainage in place, we could then finish the rest of the rain garden's expansion. The landscape fabric was covered with a thin layer of soil, and I won't put any deep-rooted or woody plants near this area, just ground covers. In the transition area between the original rain garden and the deeper addition, I set a number of rocks into the soil, being careful not to disturb the good stand of blue-eyed grass. The rocks should reduce erosion as water cascades into the deeper section.

I built a wide berm around the whole garden that's about four inches higher than the top of the blind drain. I also positioned a low point of the berm so extra water would flow out above the sprinkler head and spread into the ferns if the drainage is overwhelmed. I mulched the berm with wood chips.

I planted soft rushes (*Juncus effusus*), meadow garlic (*Allium canadense*), rain lilies (*Zephyranthes atamasca*), and blue-eyed grass (*Sisyrinchium angustifolium*) in the deeper parts of the garden. Around the edges and across the top of the berm, I planted some Stokes aster (*Stokesia laevis*) and netted chain ferns (*Woodwardia areolata*). I also planted a beautyberry bush (*Callicarpa americana*) just outside the berm. This rain garden is in dappled shade most of the day. It's worth noting that when I first established this garden, I had included cardinal flowers (*Lobelia cardinalis*) in the deeper part of the garden, but they did not last here, because this garden is not consistently moist. They worked well for my rain garden in Maryland, where there is not a seven-month dry season, but not here.

DRY WELLS

Dry wells are built to absorb and hold water. Usually, they are not visible or obvious in the landscape. They can stand alone in the landscape where water collects, or they can be combined with rain gardens or French drains to add more capacity. Most often, dry wells are constructed by isolating gravel from the soil, so the gaps between the rocks can fill up with water. To add more capacity to dry wells, you can also add larger hollows using perforated pipe, upside-down buckets, and the like. Just be sure that these items will be sturdy enough

For a dry well for our vegetable bed, Dean dug a four-by-five foot hole that was four feet deep. He kept thinking that he'd dig to the bottom of the clay, but no. So we covered the bottom of the hole with landscape fabric. Then we purchased four flexible, twelve-foot-long, perforated tubes with fabric coverings called socks. The tubes were five inches in diameter, and we connected the ends to make four donuts and stacked them in the hole. We ran more landscape fabric tucked under and around the outside of the tubes. Then we filled the hollow in the donuts with clean gravel—again left over from the former owners' projects. We laid more landscape fabric on top, used soil to filled in the gaps around the landscape fabric wrapped around the tubes with soil, and then laid in the sod that we'd cut away on top of the dry well. No one would know that it was there.

over time so they won't collapse under the weight of traffic on top of the dry-well area.

A Vegetable-Bed Dry Well

A dry well for our vegetable bed became necessary when we pulled out the lawn next to the garage to install vegetable beds there with a path between them. After our initial clearing to set up the beds, we experienced a heavy rain. For three days there was standing water on the path. We discovered that there was a thick layer of dense purple-gray clay in this area of our backyard, while most everywhere else on our property was just sandy. We needed a place for the water to go, so at the end of the path, we built a large dry well, which has functioned well for more than a decade.

A Shallow Dry Well

After more than a decade, the wood used in the platform for our three rain barrels was failing, so Dean dismantled the rain barrels and later reinstalled them on cinder blocks on the other side of the garage—with a long hose along the back of the garage so I could still irrigate the vegetable gardens. Dean reinstalled the downspout at the corner of the garage where the rain barrels had been, which created a new drainage problem.

With the barrels not there to collect the water from the downspout, and the ten-foot gutter at the back of the garage moved to the other side of the garage to fill the rain barrels in their new location, it was really soggy. But with the main pipe to the septic system and the irrigation system in the area, there were significant limitations. The solution was a shallow dry well and a path of stepping stones. I used materials on hand: cleaned volcanic gravel, broken pots, stepping stones, and landscape fabric. In another location, I might have added a rain garden, but this was too close to the vegetable raised beds.

In the space next to the garage where the rain barrels had been, I planted a new pollinator garden with plants from our yard. One can never have too many pollinators near a vegetable garden. This was also yet another project that demonstrates that landscaping is never "finished."

To make a shallow dry well, I dug an oval hole about two and a half feet wide and three and a half feet long and as deep as the irrigation cross pipe—about ten inches. The access pipe for pumping out the septic system is right next to this area. In another location, I would have made this hole bigger and deeper. I enclosed the gravel with landscape fabric, slid the drainage tray over the edge of the dry well, laid the stepping stones directly on the fabric, and covered the whole area with more cleaned gravel.

Benefits of Sequestering Stormwater

Add some rain barrels to your yard to provide untreated water for your plants and compost piles, and add some rain gardens, dry wells, or both to absorb more stormwater. These actions will help to reduce your stormwater runoff and to reduce your ecological footprint on Florida.

Resources

For more details on rain barrels and specifically our rain barrels and information on rain gardening in Florida, there are a number of articles that are listed on the resources page of my blog, www. GreenGardeningMatters.com.

There are two whole chapters on rain barrels and rain gardens with detailed instructions on sizing and installation in my book *Sustainable Gardening for Florida,* (Gainesville: University Press of Florida, 2009).

9

Container Gardening

There are many ways to use container gardens—both in small spaces on balconies or decks and also in larger landscapes. Florida gardeners can grow many types of plants in containers for various purposes, such as adding a splash of color to the landscape, extending the growing season of a crop, containing an aggressive plant that would spread too much in the garden, and of course, to soften your interior decor.

Container Gardening Guidelines

No matter what type of plant or pot, never put a layer of gravel or potsherds in the bottom. It was shown one hundred years ago that a layer of coarse material actually impedes drainage. Yet we still see various garden gurus advising people to use gravel to improve drainage. This has to do with water's affinity to itself, which I discussed in chapter 7. Water will hang together and supersaturate the soil before it jumps the gaps between the rocks. If you want good drainage, use a taller pot with a uniform soil all the way to the bottom. To keep the soil from running through the drainage holes, line the bottom with a screen, landscape fabric, or a layer of leaves, pine needles, or both. Using a fine screen or landscape fabric may also hinder ants from entering the pot. For more information on the horticultural myth of gravel in containers, see www.informedgardener.com.

Many Floridians, like this resident of St. Augustine, are limited to gardening on their balconies. While you can grow many types of plants for balcony gardens, there are also many other ways to use container gardens in larger landscapes.

The best plants for container gardens are those most able to tolerate hot soil and periodic drying. You can regulate some of this with the size of the containers. The larger containers will provide the most stability of moisture and heat. Also, the type of pot makes a difference, with clay or terra-cotta pots retaining more heat and losing more water. Double-resin pots offer the most thermal insulation. Fabric pots offer the least protection, but plants growing in them are less likely to have circling roots. I have a friend who uses old reusable shopping bags for her container gardening. The soil mixture can greatly affect the moisture retention, with sandier or lighter soil holding less moisture and soils with more organic material holding more moisture. I most often use pure compost as the soil for containers, especially for crop plants.

For long-term container gardens, refresh the soil's ecosystem with a top dressing of compost two or three times a year. If you plant more than one species in a pot, be sure they have similar needs for sun, soil, and water. For outside containers, the pot needs to be heavy enough so it doesn't blow over in a storm, but light enough that you can move it without a forklift.

Growing Vegetables in Containers

You can grow a surprising variety of crops in containers. Because late fall through winter is our best season for growing vegetables, I often add more vegetable-growing capacity by growing or starting some crops in containers. If the crop is an herb, I use a sandy soil or a sand-and-compost mixture. For other crops, I use compost or compost enriched with some composted manure as the container soil and regularly add some organic emulsion fertilizer if there is a long season.

To give my tender crop seeds such as tomatoes and peppers an early start, I plant them in flats or small pots in December. I arrange them on trays so that they can be moved inside if it's cold, but brought outside

Carrots (*Daucus carota*) and flat-leafed parsley (*Petroselinum crispum*) grow well in these eighteen-inch, double walled containers filled entirely with compost and irrigated with a hose attached to the three tandem rain barrels. These containers sit behind the garden bench next to the raised beds. After they are all harvested, the soil will go back into the compost pile.

during the warm spells to bask in the bright sun. If the seedlings outgrow their original starting pots before planting time, I plant them in temporary containers, but I work to get them in the garden as early as possible in the spring, so we can have a decent harvest before the hot, wet summer hits.

In North and Central Florida, you can use the same strategy with long-term tender crops such as pineapples. This way, you can have them outside during the warm spells but bring them inside during cold snaps.

Container Irrigation

Of all the challenges of container gardening, consistent irrigation may be the most important and is the most repetitive chore. Most people with many long-term container gardens install some type of automatic irrigation—drip irrigation or microirrigation. Self-watering container systems also help, particularly when growing crops in containers.

In order to enhance the water absorption, arrange the soil at the top of the container so that it's lowest in the middle. Irrigate only in the middle, then wait for the water to soak in. If the soil has become too dry and hydrophobic, let the first splash of water sit in that swale until it soaks in. Scratching or poking small holes in the soil will speed up the process of rewetting the soil. Follow up with additional shots of water until it readily soaks in. You don't want the water to seep down along the sides of the pot, because then it will not wet the soil.

Do a deep watering each time you irrigate—it should run out the bottom of the pot and sit in the saucer. When water sits in the saucer for a container, it will be absorbed back into the container by the soil. To control mosquitoes, dump the saucer water after a day or two. I usually dump it back into the top of that container.

Self-Irrigating Containers

There are a number of arrangements for self-irrigating container gardens, and most of them include some type of wicking from a reservoir of water stored below and separated from the soil. Most are

A friend used pairs of five-gallon buckets to create a self-watering system. The bottom buckets are screwed to a support beam, so the plants are waist high. The top buckets have a tube for filling the water reservoir and a hole sized just so the hard rim of a plastic cup will not slide through. The cup has perforations, so soil in the cup acts as a wick. The cup is put in place and the soil is loaded into the top bucket. My friend uses black plastic to cover the soil, but that is optional.

not really self-irrigating, but they do need irrigation much less often—usually once a week or so to fill up the reservoirs.

An elevated, self-watering bucket garden system has several advantages:

* It protects crops from damage by animals such as rabbits, chickens, armadillos, and pets.
* Because of the water storage in the lower bucket, the soil stays evenly moist for a week or so, depending on heat and humidity.
* It reduces water usage: Because all the water is right in the bucket, it does not drain away, and no water is lost due to irrigation onto nongrowing areas.

* It eliminates weeds and soil-based pests, such as root-knot nematodes, cutworms, slugs, and others, especially if you use purchased or sterilized soil.
* There's no bending over once everything is set up for the season. Everything is waist high.
* There's no plowing or other soil disturbance, so your underlying soil can continue to sequester carbon.

There are some disadvantages to a self-watering bucket garden:

* If you purchase new soil every year and buy seedlings from the store, this system would need to produce a lot of vegetables to offset the cost. You could reduce the cost by making your own compost to use as soil and by growing some of the veggies from seed.
* The crop selection is limited by size.
* From a climate perspective, there is a lot of plastic used, but it will last for a good number of seasons.

Containers That Need No Irrigation

If you use succulents or cacti in your containers and have them outside where they can receive rain, you will not have to worry about irrigation after the plants become established.

Seasonal Containers

I talked before about the disadvantages of seasonal plantings, where new sets of plants are installed several times a year so something is in bloom all the time. One way to more sustainably decorate your landscape with ornamental plants is to cycle through a series of containers planted with seeds or plants that will be showy for some part of the year. When those plants are blooming or have the best display, move them into a visible location, while the rest of the year they can stay out of sight until their next showy season. I admit I don't do much of this, but once in a while, it seems appropriate.

As we celebrate the holidays, so do the short-day plants. I potted two previous year's store-bought poinsettias (*Euphorbia pulcherrima*), which are native to Mexico, and kept them in natural light only. They bloomed at the Winter Solstice and became our front porch holiday décor. A Florida native, tropical sage (*Salvia coccinea*), volunteered in the pot to create an international festival of color.

Indoor Container Gardens

When we bought our house in 2004, the previous owners left us some porch plants including two pots of peace lilies (*Spathiphyllum* sp.). I guessed by their size that they were the 'Mauna Loa' cultivar—one of the more common peace lilies sold. There are about forty species of peace lilies distributed throughout tropical Central and South America. Most hybrids are derived from *S. wallisii* and *S. cochlearispathum.* They are not true lilies; instead, they are in the arum family (Araceae). These plants earned the common names of "peace lily" or "white flag" because the modified leaf, called a spathe, behind the column-shaped flower head looks like a white flag of surrender.

Peace lilies are popular, tough houseplants and office plants that thrive in relatively low light and are known for purifying the indoor air by removing toxic gases such as benzene and formaldehyde. Our peace lilies had graced our porches, but mostly we like them in the house. Some people say they need to be constantly damp, but ours were watered only once a week or so. Too much water may cause root rot. After more than four years under our care, one of our pots of peace lilies was wilting too often, had brown tips on its leaves, and the leaves had lost their typical dark green shine. When I tapped it out of its pot, I discovered it was root-bound, and this problem was compounded by the pot's being half full of potsherds in the bottom. It didn't have enough soil for holding moisture and providing nutrients.

A few months after repotting, the peace lily had filled out and was blooming. You can still see some of the yellow tips on the old leaves. The lesson here is don't use gravel or pot sherds in containers; also, remember that compost works well for both inside plants and for your gardens.

I untangled the potsherds from the roots and rinsed the roots and leaves with rain-barrel water. There was no reason to retain any of that soil—after years in the pot, it didn't have anything left to offer the plant. I added the spent soil slurry to my compost pile where it would be rejuvenated as it blended into the compost. I scrubbed out the same pot with a brush and rain-barrel water, placed a handful of leaves and pine needles in the bottom of the pot to keep the soil from running through the drainage hole, and filled the pot halfway with finished compost. I then placed the whole group of plants back in the pot, filled in around the roots with more compost, and to prevent large air spaces, added a generous amount of water as I was filling it in. I could have separated out some of the peace lilies to start a new pot, but since there was much more soil volume than before, I didn't think it was necessary to reduce the mass of plants. From what I've read, peace lilies prefer a crowded pot. I wrote a column about this adventure: "Give Peace (Lilies) a Chance"!

I Wish You Peace

Whether you have plans for growing beautiful peace lilies for your new Florida home, cultivating bountiful vegetable and fruit crops, or installing plants native to your area to replicate the Real Florida, I hope you've enjoyed my Florida gardening adventures and that you enjoy your own gardening adventures along the way. If you're like me, you'll find peace when working in your garden. As one wag put it, "Gardening is better than therapy, and you get tomatoes!"

Index

GINNY STIBOLT is a lifelong gardener, lover of the natural world, and advocate for earth-friendly practices. She earned a master of science degree in botany at the University of Maryland, but she discovered that gardening in Florida is different from her previous experiences in New England and the Mid-Atlantic regions when she and her husband moved to northeast Florida in 2004. Since then, she's been writing about her adventures in Florida gardening. In 2006, after joining the Florida Native Plant Society, she changed her landscaping style to include more native plants and more natural areas in her yard. She wrote *Sustainable Gardening for Florida* (2009), *Organic Methods for Vegetable Gardening in Florida* with Melissa Contreras (2013), *The Art of Maintaining a Florida Native Landscape* (2015), and *A Step-by-Step Guide to a Florida Native Yard* with Marjorie Shropshire (2018)—all published by the University Press of Florida. Also, she cowrote *Climate-Wise Landscaping: Practical Actions for a Sustainable Future* with Sue Reed (2018) published by New Society Publishers. She's written hundreds of articles—both print and online—for various organizations. She gives presentations to groups during her book tours in Florida. In addition, she manages the Sustainable Gardening for Florida Facebook page and writes for her own blog, www.GreenGardeningMatters.com.

Gardening should be fun. Here, Ginny shows off a garlic wreath as a fun way to dry the garlic for storage. In Florida, we grow only soft-neck garlics (*Allium sativum*), because they mature properly after growing right through the winter.